I0887052

GERMAN MOUNTAIN TROOPS 1939–42

CASEMATE | ILLUSTRATED

CASEMATE | ILLUSTRATED

GERMAN MOUNTAIN TROOPS 1939–42

YVES BÉRAUD

CASEMATE | ILLUSTRATED

CIS0020

This book is published in cooperation with and under license from Editions Memorabilia. Adapted from *Gebirgstruppen: Les troupes de montagne allemandes 1935–1945 en couleurs* by Editions Memorabilia, 2017.

Print Edition: ISBN 978-1-61200-9100
Digital Edition: ISBN 978-1-61200-9117

Design by Battlefield Design
Translate by Alan McKay
Printed and bound in the Czech Republic by FINIDR, s.r.o.

CASEMATE PUBLISHERS (US)
Telephone (610) 853-9131
Fax (610) 853-9146
Email: casemate@casematepublishers.com
www.casematepublishers.com

CASEMATE PUBLISHERS (UK)
Telephone (01865) 241249
Email: casemate-uk@casematepublishers.co.uk
www.casematepublishers.co.uk

Title page: Kampfgruppe Nord during one of its first engagements in Finland. (Luftwaffe Museum Archives)
Contents page map: The opening phase of Operation *Barbarossa*. (The History Department of the United States Military Academy)
Contents page image: Kampfgruppe Nord during Finnish operations. (Luftwaffe Museum Archives)

The author thanks Bundesarchiv Koblenz, CIRIP, ECPAD, Cahiers des Troupes de Montagne, Anciens du Maquis de l'Oisans, Ufficio Storico Esercito, Istituto Resistenza Cuneo, Gli Ultimi, Musée des Chasseurs—Vincennes, Anciens du Bataillon Berthier, Le Haut Pays, US Army, US DoD, UNADIF, Musée de la Résistance Azuréenne, Musée des Troupes de Montagne; as well as Messrs. Allain, André, Angelini, Arena, Barbi, Barkats, Bellec, Henri and N. Béraud, Casarotto, Chanel, Chassé, Contino, Davrainville, Della Siega, Demouzon, Dory, O. Duhot, Dupré, S. Ehrt, R.Eiermann, Fortier, Frondeville, Frossard, de Galbert, Gallion, Gatinel, Alain Gesgon—CIRIP, Hartmann, Hascher, Haupt, Hecht, Lagier-Brun, Le Faou, Lenz, Lissner, Lombard, Maire, Masse, Maignon, Morand, Münch, Neuner, Niklaus, Noblet, Novak, Passemard, Pecile, Pénidon, Pisano, Turinetti di Priero, Pröhl, Prudent, Rietzler, Rogger, Sabon, Sandri, Schroeder, Schubert, Simonin, Speer, Stöhr, Tabouis, Thiry, Urschiz, Vasserot, Verdenal, and Vollaire.

Contents

A reenactment of a *Gebirgsjäger*.
(www.project.edelweiss.over-blog.com)

| Author's Note

With no units specializing in mountain warfare in 1914, Germany quickly adapted to a new military dispensation: there were some significant battles in World War I with large numbers of troops in action in the mountains. These new troops distinguished themselves, and from time to time played an important strategic role, with some prestigious leaders emerging from them. In 1919, the "100,000-man army," the Reichswehr, enabled them to retain their *savoir faire* and to develop a core of experts, an "army of officers" ready to make a comeback when the time came. So it was in World War II that 15 or so mountain divisions and a plethora of smaller units came to the fore, engaged on all fronts: from the North Cape of Norway to Libya, from the Atlantic to the Caucasus, in every "hot spot" where the Wehrmacht was in action.

This account deals with the period between 1935 and 1942, and describes the life, operations, and equipment of the German mountain troops. The selection of units highlighted was made according to several criteria: the "*Gebirgs*" in the name obviously, the "mountain calling" in its widest sense, and belonging to the present-day German Federation of the Mountain Troops Associations.

The descriptions of the combat units, of their operational engagements in sectors with extreme geophysical conditions, their dress and equipment, cannot in any way be considered as an apologia for a political system. The author has not been guided by any unhealthy fascination or by the spirit of controversy. Contradictory sources have indeed been consulted, the choice in general being dictated by a return to the original sources, like the *Kriegstagebücher*, the war diaries and daily reports. This work is the culmination of 40 years of research and it could not have been written without the support of many veterans and enthusiastic collectors.

In these pages the only thing that matters is the most accurate description possible, based on the best sources, of a vast subject. A relative imbalance in how these different aspects or how the different units are treated, might be apparent to the reader. The decision to present as many images in color as possible has resulted in several problems, dealt with by using a tailored three-part approach: 1) presenting the soldiers' daily life and operations, as the specialists of extreme geophysical conditions that they were, using period photographs taken mainly at the front; 2) providing additional information on the uniforms and equipment from shots taken in museums and from private collections, inspired by period documents; and 3) offering a text giving an overall description, completed by summation tables and vivid captions.

The period illustrations in color, and the photographs or tables used for propaganda purposes are presented here for the first time, to reproduce the conditions in which the soldiers fought, but also how they trained, and how they rested. The technical quality of the photographs varies: the films—low light-sensitivity slides—were barely in circulation at the time and in general the photographers were only amateurs. The photographs in this book are mostly unpublished. A few rare shots, recently colorized, have been included for didactic purposes and to complete the presentation. The text is there to support these illustrations, in order to recreate the general atmosphere of each front as precisely as possible, knowing that photographs are rarely taken in extreme climatic and operational conditions.

Timeline of Events

With 15 divisions active during World War II, the *Gebirgstruppen*, the Wehrmacht's crack mountain troops, were to see continuous action across a wide cross-section of operations, fronts, and campaigns. From the opening shots of the war, with the invasion of Poland, mountain troops fought as far south as the Carpathians. Less than six months later, *Gebirgsjäger* were involved in the invasion of Norway where they distinguished themselves at the battle of Narvik. Then, from the frozen wastes of the Arctic Circle to the invasion of the Belgium and Luxemburg and France, mountain troops were to see action from the Ardennes to the South of France and Alsace. In April and May 1941, they were victorious again in the Balkans, Greece, and Crete, in Operations *Marita* and *Merkur*, before, finally, the seminal event of the war, the launch of Operation *Barbarossa* on June 22, 1941.

June 1, 1935: Kübler forms 1. Gebirgsbrigade, that two years later evolves into 1. Gebirgsdivision

March 12, 1938: 1. Gebirgsdivision marches into Salzburg during the Anschluss.

September 1, 1939: XVIII. Gebirgs-Armeekorps invades Poland in *Fall Weiss*.

September 20, 1939: 1.GD meets the Red Army at Lemberg/Lwow.

April 9, 1940: Operation *Weserübung*, the invasion of Norway, commences. 2. and 3.GDen land at Trondheim and Narvik.

May 9, 1940: 1.GD arrives at the Ardennes and invades Belgium.

June 8, 1940: Battle of Narvik closes with a *Gebirgsjäger* victory as Allied forces are withdrawn to the Western Front.

June 20, 1940: 1.GD crosses the Loire, then, with 6.GD prepares for Operation *Seelöwe*, until October 1940.

Gebirgsjäger watch Stukas bombing a target in the Metaxas Line, Greece, April 6, 1941.

As soon as they landed in Norway, units made their way toward the primary objectives, generally on foot since the main roads were often blocked by the Allies. Troops had to carry several days' supplies on their backs. (Ehrt Archives)

April 6, 1941: Operation *Marita*, the invasion of Yugoslavia and Greece, opens. XVIII. and XXXXIX. Gebirgskorps invade. A week later Belgrade capitulates and Sarajevo falls the next day.

April 21, 1941: With *Gebirgsjäger* having broken through the Metaxas Line, and Thermopylae Pass Greece surrenders unconditionally.

May 20, 1941: Operation *Merkur*, the invasion of Crete, commences. General Ringel's 5.GD proves critical to the relief of Student's *Fallschirmjäger*.

June 1, 1941: Germans victorious on Crete, 5.GD suffering 1,150 casualties.

June 22, 1941: XXXXIX. Gebirgskorps participates in Operation *Barbarossa*, the invasion of the USSR, arriving in record time at the Stalin Line.

June 22, 1941: Operation *Rentier* opens at Petsamo, Finland; 2. and 3.GDen victorious. Operations *Silberfuchs* and *Platinfuchs* to capture Murmansk follow, but end in stalemate.

October 8–10, 1941: XXXXIX. Gebirgskorps encircles Soviet 18th Army at battle of Mogila Tokmak (Uman, Ukraine) taking 100,000 PoWs.

May 12–28, 1942: XXXXIX. Gebirgskorps involved in the second battle of Kharkov.

Development of Germany's Mountain Troops, 1935–39

When Adolf Hitler seized power on January 30, 1933, there were no immediate changes made to the organization of the armed forces. The priorities were more economic—the country had been on its knees ever since the 1929 crisis from which it had not totally recovered, and its six million unemployed had to be got back to work—but also political and diplomatic, maintaining the status quo in Europe, reassuring the Western Powers, and renewing links with the Soviet Union which had helped with the formation of the Reichswehr.

On March 16, 1935, the law was promulgated setting up the Wehrmacht and instituting compulsory military service. The Reichswehr no longer existed. On May 21, the decree applying to military service appeared and, on August 24, fixed the period at two years.

On June 1, 1. Gebirgsbrigade was established to take operational command of the "mountain" battalions, and initial units spread over southeastern Germany. Numbers were increased by using experienced "mountain" personnel from the Landespolizei. The CO of this 1.Geb.-Brig., Lieutenant General Ludwig Kübler, was thought of as the "father" of

After the invasion of Czechoslovakia, *Gebirgsjäger* pose in front of a fortified bastion. These strongpoints were used in training, as they were similar to those on the Maginot Line, in 1940.

the new *Gebirgstruppen*. The HQ was set up in Munich in the former Bavarian Ministry of War buildings. How the brigade and its new regiments were organized was established on November 15, 1935.

The 1936 Winter Olympic Games in February allowed the *Gebirgsjäger* to give a demonstration of the *Militärpatrouille*, the forerunner to the biathlon. Organizing the event and training the German team were overseen by a staff made up of officers from the *Gebirgsbrigade* under Major Eduard Dietl.

On October 1, 1937, the brigade became 1. Gebirgsdivision (1.GD), by corresponding units being assigned to it, in particular an extra *Gebirgsjäger-Regiment* (*GJR*), GJR 98 (limited to its HQ staff) without changing its CO. In accounts of the period, this division was often referred to as the "*Alpenkorps*", a term redolent of a unit during the Great War; this created some confusion which proved beneficial in transferring traditions and developing an *esprit de corps*.

The division took part in the Anschluss, the annexation of Austria, and marched into Salzburg on March 12, 1938; then in the summer, it returned to its cantonments in High Bavaria. The World War I ally, the former Austro-Hungarian dual monarchy, or what

This young *Gebirgsjäger* photographed during the winter of 1938/9 is wearing a typical uniform of the period: a *Bergmütze* (mountain cap) with the first version of national insignia (white on light grey); a *Feldbluse* M33 (jacket) with the bluish dark green *Schulterklappen* (shoulder straps) with a light green distinctive and the first version of white on a light grey national eagle; stone-grey trousers, or *Skihose*—the quality of the photograph, one of the first slides ever used in Germany, highlights the difference between the jacket and the trousers—with buttoned pocket flaps; and *Wickelgamaschen* (puttees) made of *feldgrau* cloth. The ash skis and duralumin sticks likely come from the resort where he is spending his leave. (Reibert)

remained of it—the Republic of Austria—was thus annexed to the Reich as the "*Ostmark*" (the "Eastern Marches" of the Empire). The Treaty of Saint-Germain had left it with only a small army (the Bundesheer) of which almost half was made up of mountain troops. In it were the Alpenjäger-Regimenter 7 (AJR7, Linz), the 8 (Wels), 9 and 10 (Graz), 11 (Klagenfurt), and 12 (Innsbruck); the Landesschützen-Regiment at Hall; the Alpenjäger-Bataillone 3 (at Salzburg, with the traditions of the Rainer-Regiment 59, which wore an edelweiss during the Great War), and 4 (Bregenz).

Reorganizing the Austrian Army in 1934 had included partly redeploying some of the units and setting up two divisions of mountain troops in the Federated States of Carinthia (Kärnten) and Styria (Steiermark): the 5th and the 7th Divisions. The 5th Division was made up of the AJR 9 (Graz and Strass), and 10 (Graz), of the Jäger-Regiment 11 (Leoben, Bruck an der Mur, and Judenburg), and of the Feld-Jäger-Bataillon 9 (Judenburg); to these were added the leichtes-Artillerie-Regiment 5, the Dragoner-Schwadron 5, the Pionier-Bataillon 5, a Brigade-Telegrafen-Kompanie (brigade signals company) and a Brigade-Kraftfahrer-Kompanie (a train company), as well as a several organic units.

The 7th Division was made up of the AJR11 (Klagenfurt, Völkermarkt, and Wolfsberg) and 5 (Spittal an der Drau). The other units spread out across Carinthia were the Alpenjäger-Bataillon 1, the le.Art.-Rgt.7, le.Pi.-Btl.7, and some organic units similar to those in the 5th Division.

Edelweiss

Sleeve edelweiss: the troops' woven BEVo version (from the maker Bernd Ewald Vorsteher).

The officers' version of the sleeve edelweiss, embroidered on a dark green-blue background, adopted in May 1939.

The *Heeresbergführer* badge, a classic Wehrmacht collectible, is a rare badge by Deschler & Sohn with exquisite enameling. The two-piece *Heeresbergführer* was awarded to qualified mountain troop guides who had served actively for a year.

The sleeve edelweiss having been adopted in May 1939, that October the *Gebirgstruppen* were permitted to wear a metal edelweiss on the side of the *Bergmütze*. Its shape was new and strangely reminiscent of the one worn by Polish mountain troops; it is possible that some of the Polish ones, initially, were worn as war trophies.

This machine-gunner, or *MG-Schütze*, training on the MG 13, is wearing a trial version of the edelweiss on his *Bergmütze*.

These units were promptly incorporated into the Wehrmacht Heer after the Anschluss. They made up first 1.GD and enabled the next two divisions to be generated. Merging the 5th and 7th Austrian Divisions between April 1, 1938 and August 26, 1939 produced 3.GD with its HQ at Graz (COs Niessl then Dietl) and 2.GD at Innsbruck (CO Feuerstein) due to the addition of German units. The three divisions were placed under the operational command of the XVIII. Gebirgs-Armeekorps under General Beyer, created at the same time as the divisions. Some Germans from the Sudetenland also joined the mountain units after the invasion of Czechoslovakia and the annexation of Bohemia-Moravia in September and October 1938, an operation in which 1.GD took part. In November, the division returned to its barracks.

At the end of 1938, the peacetime order of battle (*Friedensgliederung*)

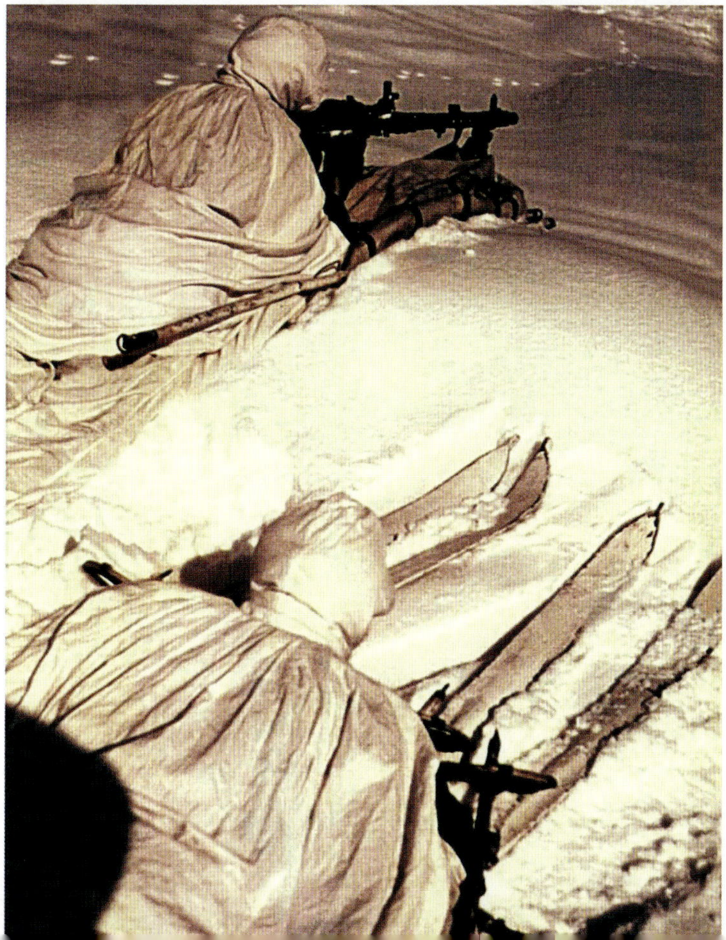

A pair of skiers, an MG 34 machine-gun team, out training wearing camouflage gear. (DR)

On parade immediately after the Anchluss: the soldiers lined up are *Alpenjäger*, recognizable by the edelweiss on the *Paroli*, the collar flaps. (DR)

boasted 51 infantry divisions already constituted or in the course of being made up, including three mountain divisions. The Salzburg Wehrkreis, the XVIII military division, was designated "*Gebirgs-Wehrkreis*" due to the fact it included two mountain divisions.

Training continued, and was even accelerated, developing cohesion in the newer units and preparing them for a conflict that was now deemed inevitable, or even sought by a number of men still upset by the conditions of the 1918 defeat.

New equipment and matériel were prepared using the experience gained during the Great War and the way in which techniques and materials in Germany, Austria, and Czechoslovakia had evolved. Our photographs enable us to appreciate the almost continuous evolution between 1935 and 1939 and how German equipment was organized, taking into account that coming out of Austria and Czechoslovakia.

A mountain guide from the Heer models different uniforms, with all qualification insignia worn on the left-hand side of his chest (instead of the right). The period colors might confuse us into believing that this man is Kriegsmarine personnel. His EK2 decoration on the chest shows that he has seen action at the front before returning as instructor. He wears an ice axe in the far right picture.

A *Heeresbergführer* displaying his climbing equipment (carabiner, pegs, climbing shoes, cords and ropes).

As a final test of Western resolve, Adolf Hitler's invasion of Poland on September 1, 1939 illustrated the blitzkrieg concept, the "lightning war" as revealed by German propaganda. The Reich's very new mountain units, with German or Austrian recruits, were all committed. Until 1945, the number of mountain units increased exponentially and were engaged on all fronts. The following chapters provide an idea of the campaigns in which the *Gebirgstruppe* took part, positioning the more significant units in their environment and in chronological order. Uniforms and equipment introduced during the war will also be dealt with, together with extraneous units.

A sergeant (*Oberjäger*) climbing instructor is belaying a *Jäger* and displays further climbing equipment (harness and rock hammer). He wears an embroidered "S" for "*Schule*" (school) on his shoulder straps.

An exercise evacuating a casualty rappeling a rockface.

A column of chasseurs from 1.GD in Slovakia, near the Polish border in early June 1939. (Moll Archives)

Poland, 1939

September 1939: the German high command left only 13 infantry divisions in the West, under the command of General von Leeb, while the bulk of the armed forces regrouped to the east with 38 divisions, among which were four motorized, five armored, and three mountain divisions. These troops were young—if in 1914 Germany had called up 25 well-trained age classes, the Wehrmacht of 1939 had only six, often formed up quickly—the result of the army being formed only recently.

On September 1, XVIII. Gebirgs-Armeekorps (Lieutenant General Eugen Beyer) rushed into Poland, as part of *Fall Weiss* ("Case White") under command of the 14th Army. With its three mountain, two infantry and one panzer divisions, the Mountain Corps' mission was to destroy any Polish forces by enveloping the southern flank, to prevent them from falling back on the Hungarian frontier. To do this, the corps was placed on the southern flank of the German dispositions.

Gebirgspioniere prepare to attack a Polish position. (DR)

Uniforms

This officer's *Bergmütze* made of fine cloth is decorated with a T-shaped national escutcheon, woven with silver.

An *Oberjäger's Feldbluse* after a few days' campaigning. The sergeant has already earned the black wound medal (one or two wounds). The dark green of the base of the *Schulterklappen* is the same as the jacket collar and greatcoat.

A visor cap belonging to a *Gebirgsjäger* NCO, made by the Salzburg hatmaker Gebrüder Hollhofer.

The *Bergmütze* with its edelweiss on a bluish-green cloth backdrop—*Abzeichentuch* (decoration cloth)—like the collar of the *Feldbluse*.

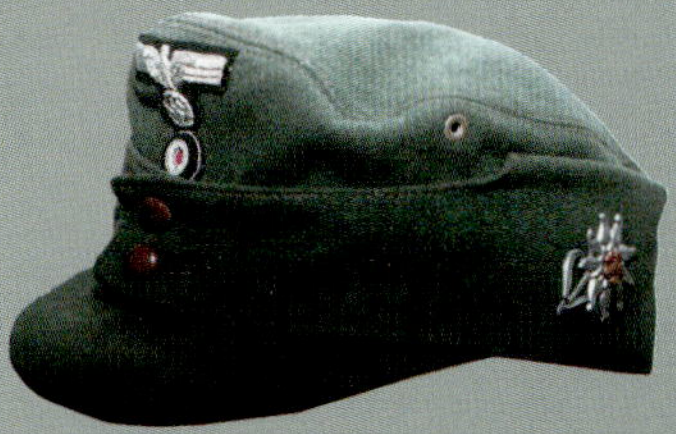

A *Bergmütze* belonging to a captain from the GJR100.

A *Feldbluse* belonging to a captain from the GJR100. The jacket bears a silver embroidered eagle and the ribbon of the Iron Cross 2nd Class awarded in Poland. Two variants of the sleeve edelweiss embroidered on a green background are presented here. As the regiment was based in Reich territory, the unit nomenclature can be attached to the *Schulterstücken*, or shoulder straps.

A column of *Gebirgsjäger* advancing near Lemberg. A twin MG 34 AA carriage is mounted on the cart. (DR)

The corps deployed to the north of Slovakia, to the east of the High Tatra, with initially the *Gebirgstruppen* in the first echelon and the motorized units following. The first objective, the pivot of the operation, was Lemberg (Lwow in Polish, today the Ukrainian town of Lviv or Leopol in Galicia), a town which had already endured bitter fighting during the Great War.

The Lightning Raid on Lemberg—*Sturmfahrt auf Lemberg*

On September 1, 1939, 3.GD (Major General Eduard Dietl) which had departed Rosenberg (Olesno) in Upper Silesia, crossed the border west of the High Tatra, toward the Western Beskids, in the general direction of Tarnow. GJR139 was detached to the 4. Leichte-Division just after the operation was launched but returned on September 5. Almost immediately on crossing the border, the division exchanged fire with defending Polish units before advancing along the Shabowka–Shosholow–Rabka axis. Geb.AA.112 and GJR138 suffered some losses on September 3 and 4 while taking Nowy Targ, Mszana Dolna, and Kasina Wielka.

2.GD (Major General Valentin Feuerstein) attacked to the east of the Upper Tatra on September 2, parallel with Biala Spiska, moving along the Dunajc, and took Nowy Sacz (Neu Sandez) then Jaslo. The enemy, partly mountain troops too (1st and 2nd Mountain Brigades, Rzezow Motorized Brigade), started delaying maneuvers to the east.

1.GD (Major General Ludwig Kübler) only came up from the Polish–Slovak border in the morning of the 5th. Its mission was to pursue and envelop the Poles to the east, advancing by train through Slovakia, an allied country, and breaking through their southern flank before taking Lemberg, a rail and road hub of importance at an operative[1] level in the rear.

For this, GJR99 (Colonel Kress), leading, attacked toward Gorlice without encountering any resistance, to ensure 2.GD's southern flank was covered. I./GJR100 (Lieutenant Colonel Rohmeder) attacked the next day, also in the direction of Gorlice, reinforced by Geb.A.A.54

1 The operative level is midway between tactical and strategic levels, at army corps-level and above.

which diverted toward Zmigdrod, reaching it on the 8th, where the rest of the division, GJR100 (Colonel Utz), which had left Ozenna in the lead, joined them.

The enemy, at this stage comprising border units, did not put up much of a fight, especially once the Magora Heights dominating Gorlice were taken. The "lightning raid on Lemberg" itself was led by the divisional motorized elements which had moved up to the front of the corps, along the main axis, with the bulk of the division coming up on foot. On September 8 the division made up a *Kampfgruppe*, Wintergest (Colonel Wintergest, commander of GAR79), organized into two *Gruppen*, Lang (commander of Geb.-P.JA.44) and Geiger (with engineers from XVIII.Geb.-AK).

Units benefitted from motorized equipment—in particular tractors for the antitank guns, indispensable for their maneuvers—making up what would be called "battlegroups" today and which would be seen again and again during the conflict. A battalion of *Gebirgsjäger* in trucks (II./GJR99, Major Seitz), elements of artillery, antitank (*PzJäger*), Flak and, of course, signals were assigned to Kampfgruppe Wintergest.

From their positions on the 8th, II./GJR98 (Lieutenant Colonel Picker), at the time in the division's second echelon, dealt with the resistance encountered around Dukla. The first intermediary objective, Sanok on the San, was taken on the 10th by the two *Gruppen*, Lang to the north and Geiger to the south. After overrunning the defenders, GJR98 (Lieutenant Colonel Schörner) captured Rowne during the night of the 8th/9th.

Gruppe Geiger ran into serious resistance on the Rymanow Heights, stormed by II./GJR99. GJR100 was hard on Kampfgruppe Wintergest's heels along the southern axis. GJR99 along the northern axis was forced to wait a while for 2.GD, stalled at Haczow, before continuing its advance. On the 10th, 2.GD, progressing eastward, crossed the San at Ruszka and Ulucz. II./GJR137 (Lieutenant Colonel Sorko) formed a bridgehead, whereas III./GJR137 (Lieutenant Colonel Matthias Kräutler) seized the important crossroads two and a half miles from the river, and GJR136 (Colonel Abin Nake) captured the heights south of Jawornik Ruski.

ID57, which had passed through Slovakia, entered Poland along the Lukow Pass. On the 10th, the two *Gruppen* from 1.GD, led by Kübler himself, finding the bridge over the San on fire, crossed the river

Gebirgsjäger from XVIII.Geb.-AK reached the banks of the San covered in dust. This *MG-Schütze* 2 (MG 34 number 2) has taken his share of the load. (Private collection, colorized photograph)

at a ford and established a bridgehead north of Sanok. Since the road toward Lemberg was opening up, XVIII.Geb.-AK ordered 1.GD to rush the objective with its motorized vanguard. Leaving Przemysl (another Great War battlefield) well defended by a powerful force, the advance resumed, and during the evening of the 11th the important road junction at Sambor was taken. The rest of the division followed in a forced march, in the dust and the heat of the end of a continental summer. On the 11th, Bircza fell without a fight. The 3rd Slovak Infantry Division was also engaged in this sector, Slovakia too having invaded Poland hoping to gain some extra territory.

On the 12th, Kampgruppe Schörner (GJR98) took the lead by recovering the main elements of the Kampfgruppe Wintergest. It continued with the attack on Lemberg by-passing the pockets of resistance left behind to slow it down, like at Rudki, which was reduced by the second echelon. On the afternoon of the 12th, Schörner entered the outskirts of Lemberg where he was greeted by heavy gunfire. The garrison had regrouped with some 20,000 troops and a hundred or so artillery pieces. But the main objective, the first part of the offensive, had been achieved: the Germans had brought up a division in the rear of the Polish defenders at Przemysl—the southern pincer was now in place. ID57 and ID7—the second echelon of the army corps—found themselves respectively east of Sanok and 28 miles south of Przemysl. 2. and 3.GDen followed in order behind 1.GD.

Kübler then deployed his forces in front of Lemberg and issued orders for the position to be held prior to taking control of the dominant Zboiska Heights to the north (to be done by the division), encircling the town to the south and southeast, and blocking off the lakeside at Grodek to prevent any reinforcements coming up from Przemysl. Fighting for control of the town began on September 13. That day, 3.GD, which arrived to the east of Sanok (Olszanica), was withdrawn from the front and sent to the Palatinate, in Germany, via Presov in Slovakia,

Thousands of Polish soldiers were captured during the offensive as seen here with PoWs watched over by *Panzerleuten* and *Gebirgsjäger*. (I.J. Haarcke Archives)

in order to reinforce the defensive positions facing France. (Inquiries conducted by HQ command after the fighting concluded that members of 3.GD had committed a number of unjustifiable acts. With little experience, they were often too nervous, ready to execute supposed partisans (*Heckenschützen*), in fact civilians who were unlucky enough to be in the wrong place at the wrong time. They also committed acts of pillage.)

During the night of the 12th/13th, considerable reinforcements were brought up in trucks from Grodowice toward Lemberg. On the morning of the 13th, I./GJR99 (Fleischmann), I./ (Franek) and II./GJR98 (Picker), as well as two heavy batteries (Art. Rgt.445) and elements of Flak and PaK, joined the vanguard. The Poles held their positions, at the same time conducting harassing artillery fire against German positions, with several shells falling close to Schörner as he was giving his orders for the attack.

At 10 o'clock, just after these reinforcements arrived, guided by a Viennese man living in the region, the Schörner group launched an attack on the Zboiska Heights, to the west and northwest of Lemberg, facing elements of the Polish 10th Cavalry and the 35th Infantry Divisions. The first objective, Hill 374, was taken by midday. The Kulikov–Lemberg road, parallel to Zboiska, the main objective of the day, was captured with measured losses. The leading battalion set up its all-round defense and drove off several Polish counterattacks on Zboiska. With Gruppe Rohmeder blocking positions to the west of the town, Lemberg found itself isolated from the bulk of the Polish defenders.

On the 13th and 14th, Gruppe Kress (III./GJR98, III./GJR99, 1./ and 16./ GJR100) in the second divisional echelon along the main axis, aligned with Kaltwasser (Zymna Voda), captured Rzesna Polska (Riasne Ruske) and the heights half a mile to the north. In the morning of the 15th, Gruppe Fleischmann (III./GJR, 1. and 16./GJR100) left their positions to prevent sorties being made east-southeast from Lemberg toward Winniki.

Meanwhile, a crisis had developed in 1.GD's rear on the 13th: three Polish divisions had been spotted by the Luftwaffe (in fact the 11th, 24th and 38th Infantry Divisions) closing in from Przemysl toward Lemberg. Kübler deployed the available motorized elements (Gruppe Zimmermann) in the morning to the Grodek corridor, between the lakes which made up a natural defense. The Polish units on foot were still between Sanok and Sambor. Gruppe Utz (GJR100 less its III./, 6 and 13./GJR99, and GAR79 less the IV./) arrived before the Polish divisions and set up defensive positions around Grodek.

There it established links with the SS-VT Germania Regiment, which had arrived out of the blue. Gruppe Utz, covered to the south by a new Gruppe Kress which had arrived from west of Lemberg, drove off violent daytime and nighttime Polish attacks, both, on the 15th and 16th.

The enemy infantry tried to regain the initiative in the forests north of Lake Drozdowicki, to the north of Grodek. The last reserves of 1.GD (13. and 16./GJR99, s.Art.Abt.445, and a motorcycle squadron from Geb.A.A.54) under the command of the division's *Ia* (Major i. G. Pemsel) counterattacked north in the direction of Dobrostany on the 16th, 17th, and in the morning of the 18th from the Jarnya crossroads. Gruppe Utz counterattacked in turn directly north, to the west of Gruppe Pemsel, then linked up with the latter together with 7.ID's vanguard. The three Polish divisions, badly mauled despite the courage of their troops, lost their resolve.

Along the route taken by this ammunition column, a *Gebirgler* examines a destroyed Polish tank. (DR)

Around Zboiska, fighting continued against some very determined Polish troops who succeeded in making several inroads into German positions but without these being in any way exploitable. On the 14th, 2.GD, together with 2. Panzerdivision, clashed with strong Polish elements around Boratycze and suffered losses significant enough to prevent it taking part in surrounding the three Polish divisions facing 1.GD in the Grodek vicinity.

The intervention of II./GJR137 and I./GJR136 (Lieutenant Colonel von Stettner) enabled the division's vanguard, III./GJR137, cut off in a powerful ambush, to disengage. The division suffered its heaviest casualties of the campaign that same day.

The vanguard from 2. Panzerdivision (which was part of XVIII.Geb.-AK) approached from the north on the Zboiska Heights on the 18th. Just before nightfall and with support from PR15 (5. Panzerdivision), GJR99 attacked on both flanks of Rzesna Polska. On the same day, the vanguard from 2.GD, GJR137 (Colonel Schlemmer), linked up with Gruppe Fleischmann, engaged in front of Winniki, XVIII.Geb.-AK thus encircling Lemberg completely.

On the 19th, the corps ordered the concentric attack on Lemberg for the 21st: 1.GD from the west and southwest, 2.GD and 57.ID from the southeast, and 7.ID from the north.

This 1.GD *Gefreiter* (Pfc) poses with Lemberg in the background, a symbolic town which his division had to retake in 1941. (Moll Archives)

Meeting up with the Soviets

On September 20, however, there was a weighty surprise: German elements at Zboiska and Winniki found themselves confronted by Soviet tanks. In turn the USSR had indeed invaded Poland on the 17th, and advanced with an overwhelming numerical superiority against the Polish Army facing west and the German invasion. Losses were sustained and talks followed the exchange of fire, with the result that 1.GD was ordered to let the Red Army take Lemberg.

On the 21st, however, the CO of the besieged garrison, who had proved his courage and operational effectiveness—his artillery in particular had caused the Germans significant losses—surrendered with his troops to 1.GD. A large part of the population tried to flee to the west before the Russians arrived.

On the 23rd, the Russians entered Lemberg according to the agreement between the two countries and the negotiations conducted by the divisional *Ia* (Pemsel)—he had initially suggested a joint Russo-German attack—as well as 2.GD.

In front of a solid rearguard, 1.GD left Lemberg for Grodek and crossed the German–Soviet demarcation line on the San near Przemysl. On the 29th, the Soviets settled on the east bank of the river, thus marking the end of the Polish campaign. (Interestingly, during 1.GD's advance into Poland, Polish Jews, members of the "Ukrainian Legion" fighting in the Sambor region under Roman Suszko, were captured and harassed: the German command noted and strongly denounced these practices. Neither do there appear to have been any Jews killed among the local populations.)

The Mountain Corps' spoils of war were impressive: 64,000 prisoners and 100 artillery pieces. General Ludwig Kübler, CO of 1. Gebirgsdivision, was the first divisional CO in the Wehrmacht to be awarded the Knight's Cross of the Iron Cross, after earning the Iron Cross 1st Class a few days earlier.

The divisions then set off back to Germany. 1.GD traveled through Slovakia by the Dukla Pass and Presov. On October 3, it reached the Rhineland. 2.GD returned via Prague, Karlsbad, Nuremberg, Frankfurt, and Koblenz to settle in the Cochem region on the Mosel. The Ahr Valley, the vineyards, and the forested areas of the Eifel enabled replacement troops to be trained and incorporated into the three divisions now based in the Rhineland Palatinate.

On September 23, 1939, German and Soviet troops meet at Lemberg/Lvov. (DR)

Norway, 1940

Unternehmen Weserübung—Operation *Weser Exercise*—was the codename attributed to the operation for the invasion of Scandinavia. Actual planning started on December 14, 1939 following a meeting between Hitler and Quisling, the former Norwegian defense minister and leader of a small nationalist party who came to embody Nazi collaboration.

The general strategy had been defined since November 1939 by Admiral Raeder: broaden the maritime front in German hands to counter the British blockade, by setting up naval support points in Norway, especially for submarines; guarantee easy access to the Baltic Sea by controlling the Straits; and control the terminal of the Kiruna (Sweden)–Narvik iron ore route, to guarantee supplies for the German armaments industry. Denmark and Norway were neutral, but were nonetheless marked down, according to Hitler's major projects, to become part of the greater German Empire, the "*Grossgermanisches Reich*." Denmark had signed a non-aggression pact with Germany in 1939 and had been called upon to allow German supply routes to transit through it. In concrete terms, where Norway was concerned, for the Heer and more especially for the mountain units, Operation *Weserübung* involved seizing key points along the coast and holding them using battalion- to division-sized tactical groups, enlarged and reinforced from Germany.

In marching columns or on motorized vehicles, moving across open terrain or through communities that might provide billets, then in the snow as they got closer to the Arctic Circle, the mountain units—here 2.GD—advanced through Norway along the iron ore route. Matériel was sometimes pulled on sledges which had been salvaged or seized, in particular the French Pourchier models. (Ehrt Archives)

A motorcycle sidecar combination travels along a fjord.

The mountain troops were mainly transported to Norway by sea. Some of the transport ships were painted in camouflage grey with large white stripes. The *Gebirgsjäger* are all wearing lifejackets of various types. (Ehrt Archives)

To gain time and outflank the enemy, transporting troops north was done using flying boats, which were very practical for landing in the fjords during the thaw. So, on May 11, 1940, 7./GJR138 arrived at Sundt, in the Elsfjord, in Blohm & Voss 138s. Junkers Ju 52/3ms were also used when landing on hard ground or frozen fjords was possible. Such aircraft were indispensable in resupplying inaccessible advanced units.

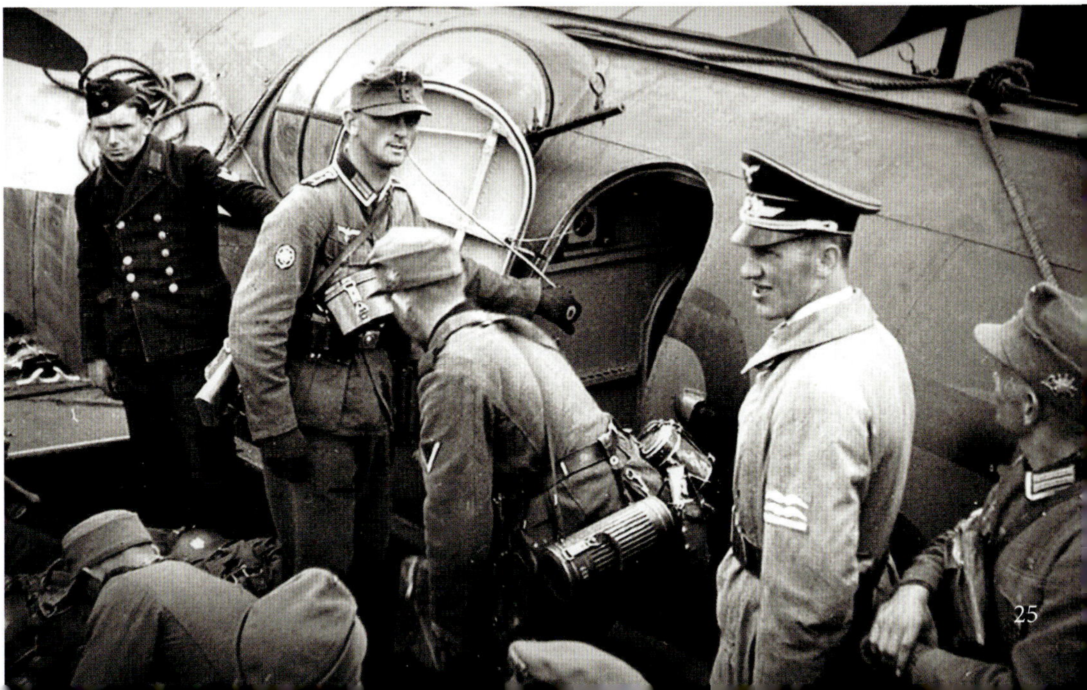

A 2.GD *Oberjäger* (sergeant) proudly poses for the camera at the port of Narvik. (Ehrt Archives)

In order to secure their advance, mountain units set up observation posts. This one, belonging to 2.GD, is armed with a Schwarzlose machine gun of Austrian origin, as was a large part of the division's armament. (Ehrt Archives)

These 2.GD *Gebirgsjäger* have adopted a practical means of moving around the fjords—a salvaged raft, with a rustic cabin. (Ehrt Archives)

For the first phase of the operation, the Germans planned on seizing seven key points in Norway but also in Denmark at the same time—"*Wesertag,*" Weser day, and "*Weserzeit,*" Weser time—by *Kampfgruppen* transported by air or sea. At the same time an infantry division and a motorized regiment reinforced by armor were to occupy Denmark (*Weserübung Süd*).

On February 20, 1940, after the *Altmark* incident when the British boarded a German auxiliary ship in Norwegian territorial waters to free prisoners held onboard, the Führer appointed a Sonderstab XXI (special HQ XXI), under the general commanding XXI.AK, Nikolaus von Falkenhorst, to start planning under the direct command of the OKW (short-circuiting the OKH), in the greatest secrecy as to the real objectives. This experience of operational planning involving all three Wehrmacht components, but without involving their respective commands, was considered successful, and therefore repeated. An example of this secrecy is perhaps best illustrated by 3.GD's inexplicable deployment toward Berlin in March, before proceeding to the North Sea ports.

The French and the British agreed on March 28 to react, and on April 8 their forces moved up by sea. A race for the common targets then began. Allied operations that were envisaged were mining the coastal waters, and seizing Narvik, Stavanger, Bergen, and Trondheim. Anglo-French attempts in Norway and Sweden at intervening in the Russo-Finnish conflict (the Winter War) had not been followed up since the Scandinavian countries refused to participate, but the troops had been prepared and equipped specifically for that operational theater, in extreme weather conditions, such as the Corps Expéditionnaire Français de Scandinavie (CEFS).

On April 9, as a (planned) reaction, the Germans issued Norway and Denmark with ultimatums through diplomatic channels: the Reich could not brook any interference by the Western Allies in Scandinavia likely to constitute a threat to its safety, German troops would remain pacific, state institutions would not be tampered with, and territorial integrity would be guaranteed, but capitulation had to be immediate. After a few skirmishes Denmark accepted the terms on the same day as the invasion. Norway refused.

According to the propaganda of the time, a *Gebirgsjäger* guards a captured Norwegian soldier. Note the canvas straps on this *Obergefreiter*'s (corporal's) helmet, frequently seen in Norway and used for attaching bits of camouflage. Slung across his back is a leather bag containing flares for a signal pistol. (DR)

The almost mythical victor of Narvik, General Eduard Dietl applied during this Norwegian campaign the principle that guided his command "*nur kein Schema*" (no scheme) or, using atypical tactics to surprise the enemy ... and sometimes his chiefs. Very close to his men, he devoted all his effort and his time to them whilst still being particularly demanding. Dietl was awarded the Oak Leaves of the Knight's Cross on July 19, 1940, the first soldier of the Wehrmacht to be awarded them.

In Profile:

General Eduard Dietl

July 21, 1890–June 23, 1944

Aged 19, Dietl joined the Bavarian Army. He saw action on the Western Front in the Great War, being wounded twice. In 1919, he joined the Freikorps, staying on in the evolving Reichswehr and Heer until war broke out in 1939. He commanded the 3rd Mountain Division (3.GD) during the 1940 invasion of Norway, lauded as the "hero of Narvik" for his skillful defense of the city. He went on to command the 20th Mountain Army on the northern Eastern Front. He was killed when the Ju 52 he was travelling in crashed near the village of Rettenegg, Styria.

General Dietl congratulating the *Vorauskommando*—the "advance party," or pathfinders—on Operation *Büffel*, at Narvik.

A 2.GD *Tross* (baggage train) crosses uneven terrain. (Ehrt Archives)

The Norwegian sites (*Weserübung Nord*) to be occupied then defended against potential British counterattacks were the towns of Narvik, Trondheim, Bergen, Kristiansand, Egersund, Arendal, and Oslo. Transport was to be by sea and at night. An airborne operation had to be organized to capture Stavanger, with Heer units following up in support. Norwegian military base camps near the targets had to be quickly neutralized.

On April 4, Colonel Hans Oster of the Abwehr communicated the date of this dual invasion to the Dutch military attaché in Berlin, as he had done for the Polish invasion, and was to do for the invasions of the Low Countries and France. No governments reacted.

2. and 3.GDen had hastily prepared themselves for the Norway operation by not deploying their motorized units and therefore their heavy weapons. Once these units landed, they would need reinforcement, by air and especially by land.

On April 6, at Wesermünde, the six destroyers from the No. 1 Naval Group (Kriegsschiffgruppe 1) intended for the operation against Narvik and the depot at Elvegardsmoen each embarked 200 *Gebirgsjäger* from GJR139 (Colonel Alois Windisch) together with the 3.GD HQ with General Dietl, as divisional commander. On April 9, *Wesertag* landed 2,000 men at Narvik. Three heavy naval vessels, the cruisers *Scharnhorst, Gneisenau,* and *Admiral Hipper*, provided protection. The crossing was complicated by a storm and 10 *Gebirgstruppen* drowned.

The naval battle that took place off the Norwegian coast is outside the scope of this study of course, but most of the German ships were sunk in the days to come and the surviving crewmembers joined the *Gebirgsjäger* and became *Gebirgsmatrosen* (mountain sailors). The high command even envisaged a general withdrawal and instructed Dietl to hold out as long as possible. Dietl quickly organized his forces, sharing the defense between the *Jäger* and soldier detachments. Narvik was taken with the Norwegian 13th Infantry Division putting up limited resistance.

A Hotchkiss H39 light tank of the 342e CACC abandoned by the French is examined by Captain Günther, an officer from the 2.GD logistics unit. Most of the photographs in this book marked "Ehrt Archives" come from this amateur photographer. Note the three-tone camouflage on the French tank. (Ehrt Archives)

Two companies from I./GJR137, hastily instructed in parachuting techniques, were dropped on May 23, 1940 into Narvik to reinforce the troops already deployed there. The *Gebirgsjäger* were issued with specific paratrooping equipment: jump helmet (*Springerhelm*, generally with two insignia), jump smock (blue-green *grummeliert Springerbluse*, nicknamed the *Knochensack*, or bone-bag), *feldgrau* trousers (*Springerhose*), and white kneepads used as gaiters. Rucksacks and group weapons were dropped in containers identified by unit markings, and which could be towed on wheels. The parachutes were stowed in a big hold-all bag after the jump. (Private collection)

On the same day, the No. 2 Naval Group brought further elements of 3.GD (200 *Gebirgsjäger* from II./GJR138, as well as the regimental commander Colonel Walter Weiss) to Trondheim (in the Trondelag region) to capture it and prepare for 2.GD's arrival.

On April 16, 1.GJR139 attacked in the Björnefell sector and took control of the railway, near the Swedish border. Dietl set up his command post in the town, on the border. But by the 17th, faced with the Allies increasingly consolidating their forces, 3.GD's situation looked precarious. Indeed, on April 14, the Norwegian 6th Division which was holding firm was reinforced by the British 24th Brigade that landed at Namsos then Aandalsnes, in order to recapture Trondheim, and then from the 14th to the 17th, at Harstad to retake Narvik. The CEFS, which had taken longer to regroup and embark its units, only landed its first elements at Namsos on April 19, being the 5^{e} Demi-Brigade de Chasseurs Alpins—DBCA. On the 20th, the Luftwaffe bombed and destroyed Namsos, a town of mainly wooden houses. Without the means to land reinforcements, the Germans decided to reembark the forces at Namsos on April 29. The Allies, faced with the beginnings of a collapse at Namsos, decided to put all their effort into taking Narvik, whose strategic worth has already been underlined.

On April 30, Allied forces prepared to move against Bjervik, to the north of Narvik. They landed there on May 13 and took it the same day.

Unternehmen Büffel and *Wildente*

Reinforcing Narvik was a constant source of worry for Gruppe XXI. 2.GD applied the second part of its plan to this once Denmark had been occupied and they'd obtained a foothold in southern Norway. On May 22, it was decided to launch *Unternehmen Büffel*—Operation *Bison*.

On May 4, General Valentin Feuerstein had II./GJR137 (Lieutenant Colonel Sorko) reinforced with 4./GAR111, transported by plane to Christiansund southwest of Trondheim, then by road to the town 125 miles away. On May 10, this *Kampfgruppe* left Trondheim and set off for the north by the only main road, No. 50 (today's E6).

On the 13th, the battlegroup reached Elsfjord, right at the end of the fjord of the same name, the end of the road after a long trip disrupted by wrecked bridges and intermittent roads, as well as skirmishing at Trofors and Eiferstraum, between the 9th and the 11th. The

Although a martial pose was *de rigueur* for the propaganda postcards showing the *Narvik Kämpfer* (the Narvik fighters), the reality was more down to earth: desperate attempts to protect themselves from the cold and the humidity, with makeshift camouflaged gear, such as tablecloths and sheets.

This NCO *mit Portepee* (with sword scabbard)—visible under the map-holder—wears a uniform that belies his section leader status. He is carrying an infantryman's Mauser Kar 98k rifle. Combing the forests was critical after any fighting. (© Festungnorwegen)

Elsfjord could only be crossed by ferry, over nine and a half miles up to Grönviken on the Hemnes peninsula. Beyond that was Finneid leading to Mo i Rana, which was captured from Norwegian elements (14th Infantry Regiment) reinforced by some 300 Scots Guards from the 157th Brigade, 52nd Infantry Division, who had arrived in Hemnes and Finneid on the 10th.

Gruppe XXI (General von Falkenhorst) decided to send a unit by plane and boat to take the enemy from the rear and make 2.GD's advance easier, in *Unternehmen Wildente* (Operation *Wild Duck*, a part of *Büffel*). The units chosen for Gruppe H were 1. and 7./GJR138 and half of 5./GAR112 (a section of two guns) from 3.GD.

Arriving at Mosjoen on May 11, Kampfgruppe Sorko saw the Anglo-Norwegians withdrawing towards the Elsfjord and embarking on cruisers that night. But *Wildente*'s primary elements (1./GJR138 and 5./GAR112) had already tried landing *en force* on Hemnesberget at the northern tip of the peninsula at around 1900, but because of the lack of surprise it therefore took place under fire from land-based British troops, then from Royal Navy cruisers that had entered the fjord. Toward midnight the situation calmed down and by the end of the night, the German positions were secured; the enemy pulled out and the advance could be resumed. The divisional HQ set itself up in the 14th Norwegian Infantry Regiment barracks.

A somewhat symbolic unit from the battle of Narvik, the *Bahnhofskompanie*, the railway station company. *Windjacke* (windjackets) have been hastily donned over the equipment because of the dreary weather. The motorbike dispatch rider is still wearing his helmet. (Ehrt Archives)

Once the fighting had stopped, the occupation began. Headquarters were set up in the various garrisons, telephone links were established, and combat units were reorganized, in particular when the planning for Operation *Barbarossa* began in early 1941. These three photographs were taken at Namsos. The officer, Captain Günther, is wearing a *Feldbluse*, cut Austrian-style. (Ehrt Archives)

Gebirgstruppen found billets in vacated Norwegian Army barracks as well as requisitioned houses; this one looks like a hunting lodge. (Ehrt Archives)

On the morning of the 12th, messages were exchanged by pennants and by *Bergjodl* (traditional songs from the German mountain regions) enabling the elements in Hemnesberget to join up with 7./GJR138 which had arrived the previous day in Sundt, two miles farther south on the fjord, by flying boat.

Gruppe H then settled into position waiting for the enemy counterattacks that were not long in coming, including naval gunfire support from British cruisers between the 11th and 13th. Because they were running out of ordnance, the Germans could not return fire. They were supplied by air at midday on the 13th. During the night of the 13th/14th, as the Allies fell back, Gruppe H took up its advance toward the strip of land at Finneid, which it captured at 1300 on the 15th after intense fighting in the snow. In the evening of the 14th, four guns from 4./GAR111 chased a British cruiser out of the fjord after scoring two direct hits—*Volltreffer*, or bull's eyes.

In order to take the Allies from the rear, II./GJR137 went round the Elsfjord by the northeast during the night of the 15th/16th, across the Neildfjell Mountains, in more than three feet of snow, on steep slopes, then over a plateau with a lake. The unit descended the Korgen Valley at 1600, then climbed up toward Finneid where it joined Gruppe H which kept watch while the *Jäger* rested. II./GJR137 then took the lead to Mo i Rana having bypassed Finneid.

The bulk of 2.GD continued its advance in the direction of Bodo by the Elsfjord and the Sorfjord. Discovering 20 or so small boats enabled them to make up an improvised ferry with lines of skiffs pulled by a British lorry, the rear deck of which was fitted out with empty fuel drums so it could float. Along the road—or rather track—that had been made impassable for the *Jäger* to traverse because of the melting snow, this machine enabled them to operate shuttles for a week in the fjord, from Gronviken to Finneid. Meanwhile 4./GAR111 continued to dissuade Royal Navy cruisers with their artillery pieces hitched up to captured vehicles and deployed as necessary.

II./GJR137 was ordered to put together a marching unit on skis—the best skiers were selected and issued with automatic weapons—so as to continue the advance during the evening of the 16th. Their mission enabled the rest of the battalion and Gruppe H, which followed at 20-hour intervals, to remain on the main axis of advance by having available a reaction unit to quickly outflank any enemy activity as it occurred. This is exactly what happened a few hours later, in front of the wrecked bridge at Stien, in the form of a well-thought-out artillery and mortar ambush by

Crossing the Arctic Circle was a photo opportunity. The *Gebirgsjäger* taking part in the Norwegian—and the French—campaign differed little from those taking part in the Polish one. (DR)

the British, along a very narrow corridor. Well-camouflaged infantry positions prevented any frontal attack until evening, and, as contact had been lost with the ski company, the German commander had to launch two companies from his *Kampfgruppe* to outflank the enemy. Hand-to-hand fighting ensued as the Scots ferociously defended their position before withdrawing toward Finneid where they fell upon the company of skiers at Mo i Rana. The bicycle section (*Radfahrzug*) was closing on the enemy as the battalion got going again and entered Mo i Rana on the 19th. The divisional staff only set off again on the 25th, toward Saltdal, near Rognan, Feuerstein himself generally just behind the leading *Kampfgruppe*.

Crossing the Arctic Circle north of Krokstand, II./GJR137 fought another skirmish to the south of Rognan on May 26 and 27. On the 30th, it had to deal with resistance around Finneid (not to be confused with the Finneid at the end of the Elsfjord) east of Fauske, after covering the section between Rognan overland, as there was no road. The Irish Guards holding the village were pounded by Stukas, coupled with the determination of the *Gebirgsjäger*.

The column was now 400 miles from Trondheim, a distance which it had covered in just 20 days. The road was in a sorry state and, after the first bridge that had been destroyed, the advance continued on foot, the baggage train transported in captured or requisitioned vehicles, which too ended up in the mire. On June 1 the column reached Grane, some 125 miles from Narvik.

Beyond Grane, there was no road, just an overland trek. The *Kampfgruppe* put together around II./GJR139 from 3.GD under Lieutenant Colonel Ritter von Hengl took the lead with a view to initially securing the Fauske–Sorfold–Bodo sector, before continuing in the direction of Narvik. By the 2nd, Fauske and Bodo were "*in deutscher Hand*."

We now turn to Operation *Bison* (*Büffel*) when Kampfgruppe Sorko on May 22 had got beyond Mo i Rana. At that date, the order setting up three "*Narvik Bataillone*" under General Falkenhorst—considering that 2.GD was spread out over almost 620 miles and that it had to regain the initiative before moving against Narvik—stipulated that the best personnel were to be picked from each unit and regrouped in one or two sections per company, one or two companies per battalion, making up the equivalent of a battalion per regiment. Apart from its organic heavy weapons—mortars, and light infantry howitzers—every *Narvik-Bataillon* was assigned an artillery section of two guns and a *Pioniere* section. Lieutenant Colonel Georg Ritter von Hengl, commander of GJR137 of 2.GD, was designated overall commander. Priority was given to these units when crossing rivers and moving up the columns.

On the 25th, all the *Narvik-Einheiten* (Narvik units) received another order, to move up in front of 2.GD from Sarfold and to deploy in the direction of Hellemobtn, and to set up the first *Stab* at Mo i Rana. There was no lack of volunteers and sometimes lots had to be drawn. Von Hengl started his mission on the 23rd, refined the axis of advance, heavily restricted as it was by having to remain out of range of the Royal Navy which had infiltrated the fjords, and by not violating the Swedish border. Sending out patrols was impossible because of the lack of time and because it was better to confront a resolute adversary quickly with a large force.

Von Hengl was able to fly over his zone of operations, as accurate maps had been handed out down to section level. It was impossible to take baggage trains—vehicles or mules and porters— so the *Narvik-Einheiten* had to travel light, advancing in 5- to 10-mile stages for 10 days or so. With air transport for logistics, this meant they had to define their areas of resupply.

The name *Büffel* (Bison) was not chosen by chance by 3.GD's operations officer, Major *i.G.* Zorn (*i.G* abbr. *im Generalstab*, or general staff officer). From the 1920s onward, within the *Gebirgstruppen* of the Reichswehr, it denoted a group of top-class skiers, calling themselves "Bisons" who afforded Captain Dietl, at the time CO of the company, the honorary title of "*Oberbüffel*." Zorn himself was a *Heeresbergführer*, from the Class of 1929–31, as was Dietl.

The first unit set off in the evening of June 3, preceded 24 hours earlier by a "technical" vanguard (*Vorauskommando*), pathfinders whose mission was more to verify the lie of the land than identify enemy positions. The terrain was notable for its cold humidity: melted snow, fjord water, thawing moorland, and lakes at altitude. The least unpleasant place was crossing the Gicecocca glacier, which was solid "ground." But volunteers can put up with anything especially if it was a question of "reach Narvik." Thirty *Vorauskommando* men, bearded with deep-etched features, reached Narvik on June 13 but the end of the hostilities on the 10th had rendered Operation *Büffel* null and void even though it had been fulfilled.

The Battle of Narvik

On May 23, two companies of I/GJR137—1. and 2.Kp.—made up of volunteers trained to become parachutists in 10 days, were dropped into Narvik to reinforce the mountain and parachute units already in position and under great pressure from the Allies. Initially they made up the reserve to intervene immediately should an Allied landing take place, before deploying respectively to the tunnels at the Iron Ore Route terminal and Ankenes, reinforcing 8./GJR139.

May 27 heralded the opening of operations in the Narvik sector. French and Polish forces had seized the approaches over two weeks of intense fighting. Shortly before midnight, the British fleet opened the bombardment against defensive positions installed to the north of the town. The first troops landed at 0015, in all two battalions of the 13ᵉ Demi-Brigade de la Légion Etrangère (DBLE) in two waves two hours apart, from the north—they had been landed at Bjervik on the 13th. They took the village of Orneset, northeast of Narvik, then expanded the bridgehead westward and by dawn, reinforced by 500 men, eastward along the "Iron Ore Railway" line.

The *Narvik Schild* (shield) was the first commemorative shield to mark the participation of the German armed forces in a campaign. The example shown here is the Heer model, fixed on a piece of *feldgrau* cloth by four hooks reinforced by an iron counter-plate. It was sewn on the top of the left-hand sleeve. Only personnel of the three armed services (and a few Merchant Navy civilians) could be awarded it, and only if they'd been engaged in the Narvik sector, as defined by the Commanding General Gebirgskorps Norwegen on September 9, 1940, together with the precise criteria for its being awarded and endorsed by Dietl as the former *Befehlshaber Gruppe Narvik*. The shield was created by Professor Richard Klein in Munich. In all, 8,577 were awarded, 670 posthumously. They were delivered late—the first 10,000 units were stuck on a ship locked in by ice in the port of Stettin—and only after General Dietl had received his from the Führer himself on March 21, 1941.

On the German side, the Royal Navy artillery barrage disrupted communications, heralding difficulties in coordination between the sailors, who bore the brunt, and the *Gebirgsjäger* in terms of operational planning. Another French unit coming from the north of Öjord on the shores of the Herjangenfjord, landed at 0615 at Taraldsvik, the northern quarter of Narvik, with three Hotchkiss H39 tanks, one of which got bogged down on the beach in front of 6./GJR139 before being neutralized by a 2cm Flak gun.

The enemy advanced with difficulty through a very steep, wooded area, enabling 6./GJR139 to form a defensive line. At the same time, 8./GJR139 was under attack by the Polish Podhale Chasseurs at Ankenes on the other side of the Beisfjord, where the Poles had landed on the 28th. In order to avoid being taken in the rear by the 13ᵉ DLBE closing the second arm of the pincer, 6./GJR139, suitably dispersed, was able to block the legionnaires on the slopes of the Fagernsfjell, to the south of the Taraldsviken stream.

The Royal Navy again began bombarding the town between 0400 and 0500. At 0647, Major Haussels (II./GJR139) ordered the almost-encircled 150 *Gebirgsjäger* and 250 sailors in Narvik to fall back eastward and to set up defensive positions in the mountains. After several weeks of preparation and one night of fighting, the termini of the Iron Ore Route (Norwegian Corridor) had fallen into Allied hands. From May 29 to June 4, the Allied offensive continued in the direction of the Swedish border. The Franco-Anglo-Norwegian forces outnumbered the Germans, and were well equipped and motivated. The fighting was intense, in difficult climatic conditions with German resupplies sporadic, either via Denmark or by sea. The conflict was to last two months with no decisive outcome.

Dietl had envisaged crossing into Sweden, a neutral country, to be interned there with his unit—near Narvik, the border is less than 31 miles from the sea—but on the 24th, because of the situation in France, the joint Anglo-French command decided to implement Operation *Alphabet*: the withdrawal of the Allied forces. After destroying the port and railway installations, the Anglo-French expeditionary force began reembarkation on June 6, leaving the Germans to savor a walkover. On the 10th, Norway finally capitulated.

At the end of the battle of the Iron Ore, 2. and 3.G.Den remained in Norway as the occupying force. *Weserübung* had caused heavy losses in the Kriegsmarine, limiting the success of this operation but the Germans retained control of the Baltic and its access. The major strategic objective had been achieved: the Iron Ore Route continued to work for the benefit of the German war effort. Without Swedish iron ore, the British estimated that Germany would only have been able to hold out for 12 months. Finally, the impact of this was important from a political and propaganda viewpoint: against an Allied force almost six times stronger, the Wehrmacht had won the day, giving added credence to its reputation of invincibility, which the French campaign went on to cement.

German soldiers killed in the fighting in Norway were first buried *in situ*: witness this "military square." The inscriptions on the beautifully carved stone tell that these soldiers "fell for Greater Germany in 1940." Civilization returns when tributes are paid to the dead and at Narvik the Germans, no doubt with the help of prisoners, established a military cemetery for those killed from the 13ᵉ DBLE (Demi-Brigade de la Légion Etrangère). (Ehrt Archives)

On May 9, 1940, 1.GD set off from its garrison in the Rhineland in marching columns, entering Luxembourg and then Belgium. This section is part of GJR100. (© CIRIP, Alain Gesgon Collection)

France, 1940

XVIII.Geb.-AK and 1.GD were the only mountain units to wholly take part in the French campaign. The troops had recovered from the Polish campaign to the Rhineland where the Rhine and Ahr valleys, and the Eifel Mountains provided an ideal training environment, the Eifel Mountains particularly offering good, "harsh" training potential. The division, in XVIII. Gebirgskorps, came under commander *General der Infanterie*, General Eugen Beyer, and chief of staff Colonel *i.G.* Hubert Lanz.

Blocked for a fortnight below the Chemin des Dames, 1.GD endured sustained accurate French fire. Here an MG 34 team and an artillery observer in a swamp peer cautiously to their front. (Private collection)

At dawn on June 5, 1.GD was able to resume the offensive on the Aisne and the Ailette, a phase illustrated on this propaganda postcard with an edelweiss, showing the first assault wave of *Gebirgsjäger* and *Gebirgspioniere* on a *Schlauchboot* (inflatable dinghy). (Private collection)

Under the command of Field Marshal von Rundstedt, the army group had to break through the natural obstacle of the Ardennes with its armored units, cross the Meuse at Sedan to overwhelm the main French forces from the south and cut them off, in Operation *Sichelschnitt* (scythe stroke).

On the 9th, shortly after midday, 1.GD was ordered to set off. It reached the Belgian border having traversed northern Luxembourg on foot, preceded by a motorized vanguard commanded by Colonel Ferdinand Schörner (commander GJR98). Initially planned as an offensive crossing in front of well-armed French forces and over difficult terrain, General Kübler realized that the enemy, outflanked by the panzer divisions and harassed by the Stukas, had broken off any potential engagement. The bulk of the division therefore advanced across pontoon bridges constructed by the *Pioniere*—the French had destroyed all the bridges in their retreat—and crossed the Meuse at Revin and Fumay, during the night of May 14/15.

The first contact with the enemy was made on the 17th at the edge of the Signy and Saint-Michel forests. The few French tanks that took the *Gebirgsjäger* to task were destroyed or driven off by the PaKs, and several hundred prisoners including a general were captured when the woods were cleared. However, the division suffered its first losses of the campaign.

The following phases would bring back memories of World War I.

After a day's rest on the 18th, the division was rushed to the Oise-Aisne Canal and the Ailette river, to the south of Coucy-le-Château, in order to cover the southern flank of the army group. The French, who were well aware of the risk of encirclement by the Germans when they broke through at Sedan and Hirson, initially held both banks. The fighting was heavy: the French held their ground; their artillerymen had excellent observation posts on the southern heights (the western end of the Chemin des Dames); the marshy zones that were

At dawn on June 9, *General der Artillerie*, General Ritter von Speck, commander of XVIII. Geb.-AK went up with his staff—whose chief, Colonel Lanz, can be seen here—to the top of Soissons Cathedral. A staff officer brandished a *Fliegertuch* to signal the troops' advance to the Luftwaffe. The general was applying an OKW directive dated December 18, 1939 stipulating the use of swastika flags as recognition signals. (Moll Archives)

On June 15, General Kübler ordered his division to wear the *Siegesbruch*, the bunch of victory oak leaves, for three days. This was more of an Austrian tradition—a regulation version made of synthetic material existed. The soldiers of 1.GD, however, preferred natural leaves. (Private collection)

The "100er" approaching the River Loire, on June 18. At the village of Chantecoq in the Loiret, officers are asking directions from rather wary residents. Most of the CIRIP photographs of the French campaign and the Balkans seem to have been taken by, or for, the officer with a white neckerchief holding a map. He is wearing a camouflage loop (*Schlaufe*) over his *Schulterstücken* (shoulder boards). (© CIRIP, Alain Gesgon Collection)

infested with mosquitos bordering the double watercourse provided excellent opportunities for enfilading fire, and made any advance extremely difficult, even by night. 1.GD established defensive positions along a 20-mile front, having suffered heavy losses.

But, as was often the case during the French campaign, it was pressure from other sectors that had an impact on one particular sector of the front. Operation *Dynamo*, evacuating the British Expeditionary Force and several French divisions from Dunkirk, had marked the first part of the campaign and played havoc with the overall French defense. After more than two weeks being blocked, 1.GD changed subordination on June 2, from XVIII. to XXXXIV. Armeekorps, on the eastern flank of the 6th Army and resumed the offensive at dawn on the 5th. Along a front which had shrunk by five miles, it attacked with two regiments in the lead, GJR100 on the right and GJR99 on the left, backed by 11 artillery groups, between Pont-Saint-Mard and Crécy-au-Mont, faced by the French 93ᵉ RI (Infantry Regiment) of the 7ᵉ DI (Infantry Division).

III./GJR99 did not succeed in crossing the watercourse in its sector but in the evening, the Chemin des Dames heights were taken, as the Germans outnumbered their enemy threefold in a struggle against stubborn opposition—well-protected French units and persistent, effective artillery, just as the veterans of the Great War recalled—with significant German losses (500 casualties, the heaviest of the campaign). GJR98 had intervened at the pivot with its neighboring division to the north and overwhelmed the 93ᵉ RI to take Juvigny. The spoils were large. On June 6, the breakthrough continued to the Aisne, with two leading regiments reaching the river toward 0800. GJR98 was faced with a French counterattack aimed at rescuing the 93ᵉ RI HQ near Juvigny. II./GJR99 (Major Seitz) secured a bridgehead before nightfall. The general breakthrough by the German forces in this sector obliged the French (17ᵉ Corps d'Armée) to break off to the south of the Aisne. On the 7th, the army corps gave Kübler's division a day's rest.

On the 8th, the division resumed its advance toward the Aisne, and crossed the river near Soissons without encountering any significant resistance. The Luftwaffe dominated the skies and intervened to discourage any ideas the French might have of counterattacking. The French Air Force acted mainly against the river crossings and managed to hamper the advance of support echelons and baggage trains. Advancing was difficult: the summer heat wore out the *Jäger* whose woolen cloth uniform was unsuitable. But compared with the French who were wearing greatcoats, the Germans could at least roll up their jacket sleeves. Liaison by radio was problematic, the technical capabilities of sets being limited and distances proving excessive in a spread-out, almost continuous war of movement.

In the early hours of June 9, *General der Artillerie*, General Hermann Ritter von Speck—only in post since June 5—and his XVIII.Geb.-AK staff climbed to the top of the tower of Soissons Cathedral in order to hoist the German flag. Using a *Fliegertuch*, his aim was to mark the progress of his corps to the Luftwaffe, to avoid the Germans destroying the edifice once again. He was killed at Pont-sur-Yonne on June 15, alongside several of his troops, the first general to be killed in combat in World War II.

During the evening of the 9th, the division advanced along the Ourq in the Vichel region with its three regiments. GJR100 established a bridgehead, enabling the bulk of the division to cross the next day despite being harassed by enemy artillery.

On June 19 the "98er" tried to enlarge the bridgehead at Gien, begun the previous day by Vorausabteilung Lang and 3./Radfahr-Abteilung 403. (© CIRIP, Alain Gesgon Collection)

On June 10, Italy declared war on France and Paris was declared an "open city." 1.GD took part in the large outflanking maneuver around the French capital from the east. After a simple order from General Kübler (*Die Truppen haben freie Bahn im Wettlauf zur Marne*—the troops have an open road in the race to the Marne, the fateful river of 1914), the river was reached at Château-Thierry in the evening of June 11. The objective: provide solid bridgeheads for the armored units to break through toward the south, by preventing the enemy from establishing his lines of defense. During the morning on the 12th, 1.GD crossed the Marne. The same day, General Weygand, now aware that the battle was lost, decided to establish a defensive line backing onto the natural obstacles of the Tours-Dijon line on the eastern border (Maginot Line, Upper Rhine, Vosges). The number of French units breaking off and pulling back was increasing and the Germans encountered only weak resistance, overrunning depots and strongpoints abandoned intact. The race had started, by companies in columns, mostly on foot.

On June 14, the Wehrmacht paraded in Paris. The same morning, the division formed a motorized vanguard (*Vorausabteilung*) unit under the command of Geb.-Panzerjäger-Abteilung 44, Lieutenant Colonel Lang, who had already distinguished himself in Poland in this type of operation. The marching troops reached the Seine to the south of Provins where a panzer division was crossing a bridge which had been taken intact; it was ordered to sheer off to the southwest and establish a bridgehead in the region of Balloy and Bray-sur-Seine. The French had blown all the bridges and crossings over the Seine. It was a spectacle of total desolation: abandoned matériel, isolated soldiers, refugees, all piled up in front of the bridges. Without stopping, the division went through Bray and crossed the river over a pontoon bridge which had been thrown across it. On the 15th, in recognition of the effort made by his troops, Kübler ordered the *Siegesbruch*—a bunch of oak leaves—to be worn on the *Bergmütze* for three days, to signify victory.

On June 16, the division resumed its advance beyond the Seine and the Yonne, with a new objective, Gien, on the Loire, 100 kilometers farther south, in order to take the crossing points.

On the 17th an important development occurred: the 1st Army in Lorraine and the 7th Army in Alsace at Colmar broke through the Maginot Line at two points, along the axes of the secondary attacks as the leading panzers reached Tours in the Loire Valley and the Swiss border in the Pontarlier and Belfort region.

France then sued for peace and the Reynaud government withdrew, leaving Maréchal Philippe Pétain in charge. Vorausabteilung Lang was ordered to make a dash to Gien, via Chéroy-Ervauville and Montargis, at midday, bypassing any pockets of resistance and without concern of outstripping neighboring units. The advance was only delayed by Stuka bomb craters, the carcasses of dead horses, and wrecked vehicles, in the midst of increasingly dense floods of refugees.

A few miles before the town, backed by howitzers from IV./GAR79, flanked by PaKs that were dealing with the French armor trying to intervene, and picking up the elements of 81.ID, Lang neutralized a French unit that was trying to stop him; he ended up reaching a town in flames, in crowds of refugees terrorized by the fighting taking place all around them, amidst explosions and screams of terror. The 3./Radf.-Abt.403 motorcyclist company assigned to Lang as reinforcement, managed to cross the partly destroyed bridge. By the end of the evening Lang had established a narrow bridgehead which the detachment managed to broaden the following morning; in the end, mission accomplished perfectly. Lang had captured several thousand prisoners, and had destroyed or taken 700 armored vehicles and 150 artillery pieces.

On the 18th, Kübler hurried to Gien to assess the situation for himself after he'd rounded up a battalion from GJR98 in trucks from the Chacelles region to consolidate the bridgehead. However, the French units holding the southern bank of the river put paid to any ideas of a bold raid. The bulk of the division picked up speed, undisturbed by enemy aircraft. On the 19th, in the morning, reconnaissance along the southern bank continued before reports started coming in revealing that the enemy had withdrawn. Little by little the "98er" infiltrated on inflatable rafts, bypassing the remains of the road and rail bridges. The following day, the rest of the division followed on ferries whilst the *Pioniere* were busy building a pontoon bridge that was completed by evening. GJR98's motorized troops, after finding a breach in the French defense, resumed their advance toward the Cher, arriving

In the evening of June 20, the bulk of 1.GD was able to cross the Loire over the pontoon bridge the engineers had built that day. (© CIRIP, Alain Gesgon Collection)

Although the motorized elements and the divisional staff were able to quickly reach Lyon on June 21, the rest followed by road. GAR79 advances on foot here with its 7.5cm Geb.Geschüzen 36. The howitzers were drawn by mules or horses. (DR)

between Mehun-sur-Yèvre and Quincy during the day. But a new situation had developed which Kübler immediately acted upon. On June 21, while it was taking a well-earned rest, 1.GD was ordered to force-march southeast, in the general direction of Lyon where 3. Panzerdivision was indeed blocked in front of Grenoble, near Voreppe, trying to take the Groupe d'Armées des Alpes in the rear.

This was to support an Italian maneuver which failed to break through the French defense along the border (Alpine Maginot), a failure which the *Gebirgsjäger* found amusing. Only the *Stab* had reached Lyon when the Armistice was signed on the 24th, to come into force the following day at 0635.

On July 4, at the end of the campaign, 1.GD regrouped in the Jura Mountains along the Swiss border where it watched over the demarcation line. It took advantage of the favorable environment to resume mountain training. Following the plans stipulated on July 2 by order of the Führer, the *Gebirgsjäger* left the Alps to prepare for Operation *Seelöwe* (Sealion)—the invasion of Britain—in the Caps Blanc Nez, Gris Nez, and le Touquet sectors where they could train in conditions specific for climbing and amphibious maneuvers. On October 12, the operation was called off and the division returned to the Swiss border, its *Jäger* puzzled by this "*Gebirgsmarine*" experience.

In December, in the Besançon area, under the command of XXXXIX.Geb.-AK, 16,000 mountain warfare specialists began training for Operation *Felix,* the proposed invasion of Gibraltar and its British fortress. Major General Hubert Lanz, recently promoted and commander of 1.GD since October 25, succeeding Kübler who now commanded XLIX. Geb.-AK, would lead the operation. He spent many hours poring over a 1:1,000 model of the Monkey Rock (Gibraltar) which had been especially made. The operation was put off indefinitely at the beginning of February 1941. The division was then distributed across the Doubs (Besançon) Department.

1.GD was joined at the front in June by 6.GD, recently formed at Innsbruck. Indeed, Colonel Ferdinand Schörner left his post as commander of GJR98 of 1.GD after the fighting on the Ailette, to be appointed commander of the new division by the OKH on June 1. On the 2nd, he was ordered to establish the division, to be ready for the 10th with a small group of officers—limited at first to his operations officer, Captain Georg Gartmayr, previously a 1.GD staff officer. The assigned units would gradually filter in from all corners of the Reich, including the Ostmark (Austria since the Anschluss), and equipment was to be issued from wherever it could be found in Germany. Two companies were in quarantine because they were ill, so one can imagine the difficulties in assembling the new division. Moreover, the bulk of the unit was made up of reservists with no combat experience. Cohesion was out of the question. The incomprehension of such a precipitous decision—a first in the history of the German army—was understandable. Initially, only GJR141 was in residence at the Döberitz camp, where its tardy preparations had prevented it from joining Dietl in Norway.

On the 10th, most of the division, 17,188 men, was assembled at Heuberg camp in the Schwabisch Jura; what was now needed was to turn it into a combat weapon and a mountain one at that. 6.GD therefore left on foot toward the Rhine on the 12th, crossing part of the Schwabisch Jura and the Schwarzwald, accessing the western reaches on the 17th. The march was used to improve training and cohesion. With the Vosges Mountains visible with three enemy army corps situated on the crests, the Maginot Line garrison troops were ordered to withdraw on the 14th, the date of the Germans' arrival in Paris. The new division was ordered to stand fast in the staging area (*Verfügungsraum*) where it was able to perfect its training and where, at the same time, the pressure on the commander tapered off.

However, on the 19th, the order came through for the division to move off to the Vosges; the reconnaissance unit crossed the Rhine followed by the rest of the division. During the night, the division regrouped at Sélestat, taken on the 17th and where the divisional staff was planning for an engagement. The following morning, under XXV.AK's orders, 6.GD endured its baptism of fire in the Vosges. The attack was carried out along two axes: GJR143 along the valley of Villé via Thanvillé, Saint-Martin, toward Bourg-Bruche, Saales, and Orbey to the south; and GJR141 via Andlau, le Hohwald toward Waldersbach to the north, with *Jäger* or *Aufklärer* (whom Schörner called "*Reiter*", riders) reinforced by tank destroyers as a vanguard. The troops were keen to prove their worth and rushed forward looking for any opportunity to contact the enemy. But the French, well dug in and well supported by artillery, held on despite being discouraged after pulling back from the Rhine.

Along the southern axis, 200 men were wounded or killed. Schörner was constantly present among his troops, applying Clausewitz's principle of commanding from the front, and his concept of maneuver: brutality and speed. His Pour le Mérite Cross, awarded during the Great War, sparkled in the sun, as his *Jäger* later testified. The division was allocated a neighboring infantry regiment as reinforcements.

On the 21st, the division continued to forge ahead, Schörner having expressed his intention of overwhelming Saint-Dié in order to capture or destroy as many of the enemy's forces as possible. Bruche, la Grande Fosse, Moyenmoutier, Senones, Saint-Blaise, and Saales were all bypassed, the defenses swept aside, as the "hunt"—the term used in these circumstances—continued. On XXV.AK's orders, Schörner raced ahead with a small escort (an artillery lieutenant colonel and his operations officer) to Saint-Dié in the morning of the 22nd to negotiate the capitulation of French forces engaged in the sector. With GJR143 blocking the northern exits of Saint-Dié, and artillery ranges zeroed, he appreciated the weak combat circumstances of the enemy. He demanded General Condé's 3e Armée surrender unconditionally by 1500. To avoid heavy losses and conscious that his overall strategic situation was catastrophic, that his own troops were exhausted, scattered, and barely motivated, Condé acceded. The rest of Stab 6.GD joined its commander and settled in in the Nouvel Hôtel in front of the Saint-Dié railway station.

In Profile:
General Karl Hubert Lanz
May 22, 1896–August 15, 1982

Lanz joined the army just before the outbreak of the Great War, serving on the Western Front. He stayed on in the much-reduced Reichswehr into the 1930s. As Chief of Staff XVIII Corps, he received the Knight's Cross for his role in the battle of France. He commanded the 1st Mountain Division (1.GD) during *Barbarossa*, seeing continuous action into the *Fall Blau* campaign. In June 1943, he took command of XXXXIX Mountain Corps in the Crimea. Virulently anti-Nazi, he was involved in plans to liquidate Hitler, but somehow escaped the noose. In late 1943 he assumed command of the XXII Mountain Corps in the Balkans. He was found guilty of war crimes at Nuremberg—for the Cephalonia and Corfu massacres—but served only three years of a 12-year sentence.

On June 22, Lanz was slightly wounded while observing the capture of Oleszyce by GJR98. He is being attended to by Dr Sebald and Sergeant Moll, one of his dispatch riders, while Lieutenant Stredele, his aide-de-camp, holds the map for him. His *Stab* was set up as close as possible to the frontlines, at Judengraben. (Franz Moll Archives)

General Lanz decorates a *Gefreiter* with the Iron Cross in front of his section leader, for destroying a T-34 at close range. (Franz Moll Archives)

Up until the 24th, the day the Armistice was signed, skirmishes with French units, spread out over difficult terrain, continued. The division then had to deal with the 100,000 prisoners from the 3e, 5e and 8e Armées, which were transported across the Rhine to Germany. Just like 41.GD, the division was then transferred to Normandy to prepare for *Seelöwe*, before onward transfer to Styria in the Semmering Mountains of southeastern Austria. Schörner was promoted to lieutenant general on July 18.

Feelings across the Wehrmacht were the same: the honor of the German Army, beaten in 1918—because it had been stabbed in the back by the politicians—was restored, with "Compiègne 1940" negating "Compiègne 1918" with God once again on the side of the Germans. The motto "*Gott mit uns*" (God with us) inscribed on the soldiers' belt plates seemed once again to be justified. The rise to prominence of the *Gebirgstruppen* continued apace, while fighting in the west and northwest continued.

At the end of the summer, four *Gebirgsdivisionen* (*GDen*) had already been constituted, together with the four staffs for the mountain corps (Gebirgskorps Norwegen, XVIII., XXXVI., and XLIX. Gebirgs-Armeekorps). During the fall two new mountain divisions were established: the 4th in the Schwabisch Jura and Württemberg under the Austrian General Eglseer; and the 5th in Bavaria, where it recovered GJR100 (Colonel Utz) from 1.GD, under the Austrian General Julius Ringel.

Four *Jägerdivisionen* (97, 99, 100, and 101) were added to the *GDen* above, in effect four large units of light infantry more or less thought of as "*gebirgsfähig*" (apt for combat in "medium mountains" or "difficult terrain"). These divisions will be dealt with later. At the beginning of 1941, a mountain division was also constituted within the Waffen-SS, the 6.SS-Gebirgsdivision Nord, deployed in Norway, at the outset the size of a regimental *Kampfgruppe*. This brought the strength up to four army corps and 11 specialized mountain divisions, in preparation of the imminent campaigns.

The 6.GD's offensive was brief but intense, but it captured a lot of prisoners and matériel. "*Das ist der Sieg*" (this is victory) was the caption for such images.

The Balkans and Crete, 1941

After the ill-advised idea of invading France in June 1940, Italy decided to restore its image by attacking Greece, a country Mussolini thought was weak and divided. On October 28, after a few diplomatic "incidents," Italian forces violated Greece's neutrality by attacking it from inside Albania which she had occupied since early 1939. Within a few weeks, the Greeks had driven the Italians out and even penetrated 37 miles into Albania. Hitler was obliged to come to the rescue.

Two mountain corps took part in the Balkan campaign: XLIX. Gebirgskorps, including 1.GD, subordinated to the 2nd Army given the task of attacking Yugoslavia, Belgrade in particular; and XVIII. Gebirgskorps with 5. and 6.GDen. 4.GD was attached to XIV. Panzerkorps; moreover, II./Regiment Brandenburg units engaged in this theater wore the *Gebirgstruppen* edelweiss.

On January 11, 1941, Hitler signed *Weisung Nr. 22* (directive No. 22) for the Heer and the Luftwaffe, stipulating how Italy was to be supported in North Africa and Albania.

Leaving their temporary quarters in France, 1.GD began their deployment by train. Regimental planners showed some imagination with this meal area out of a wagon, in which were set up the "*Gulaschkanonen*" ("goulash cannons"), the nickname given to the *Feldküchen*, the field kitchens. (© CIRIP, Alain Gesgon Collection)

The Bulgarian authorities made a point of showing their loyalty to their German ally in the villages the troops passed through en route to the front. (© CIRIP, Alain Gesgon Collection)

While preparatory plans for Operation *Barbarossa*, the invasion of Russia, were forging ahead, the powder keg that was the Balkans posed a dangerous threat to the southern flank of the Axis Powers. To subdue the region, the 12th Army under General List attacked Yugoslavia and Greece in early April 1941. Along the Metaxas Line, 5. and 6.GDen experienced the hardest fighting that the *Gebirgsjäger* and the Wehrmacht had experienced until then.

By mid-November 1940, Italy's failure in Greece and the subsequent British occupation of Crete brought back memories of the Greeks' unpredictability in World War I, which made them potentially suspect. On November 23, Romania joined the Tripartite Pact, thus augmenting the cordon sanitaire to the north of the

Regulation carts or those lent by the Bulgarians followed the combat units. Note that the driver of the first cart is wearing a *feldgrau* greatcoat, probably one of the earliest to be issued. (© CIRIP, Alain Gesgon Collection)

A company pauses by the side of the road in Bulgaria. (© CIRIP, Alain Gesgon Collection)

peninsula. In December, one of President Roosevelt's special envoys, Colonel Donovan (the future chief of the OSS, the forerunner to the CIA), was sent to Greece to warn of an imminent attack by Germany. In early February, the late Prime Minister Metaxas was replaced by Alexandros Koryzis.

On March 2, 1941, the Germans entered Bulgaria again to "reinforce the links" with Sofia. In response to what they considered an occupation in disguise, the British opened Operation *Lustre*: 58,000 soldiers were deployed to Greece between March 4 and 7.

In order to show that they were not there just to fight, the *Gebirgsjäger* had their *Musikkorps* give open-air *aubade* concerts or *Platzkonzerte* along the route. The bag containing the scores, hooked to the belt, was inspired by the map holder from the Great War. When wearing campaign dress, the musicians did not necessarily wear the distinctive swallows' nests (*Schwalbennester*) on their shoulders. (© CIRIP, Alain Gesgon Collection)

GJR100 advanced along dusty roads, coming across Bulgarian troops from time to time. The "all-purpose" trailer in the center is a *schwerer Heeresfeldwagen* (*Hf.2*), a heavy army field wagon, followed by requisitioned matériel. (© CIRIP, Alain Gesgon Collection)

These *Jäger* have found a photogenic subject on the roadside. The unit on the road is a mortar section; the metallic ammunition cases attached to the pack saddles are visible. The *Jäger* on the right is carrying a small backpack which was not regulation mountain gear. (© CIRIP, Alain Gesgon Collection)

Officers on horseback. The company commander prefers *feldgrau* stockings to puttees and ankle supports. (© CIRIP, Alain Gesgon Collection)

Photographs of the essential element for keeping horses and mules in good shape are rare: the blacksmith and his field forge. This scene was photographed in Bulgaria as troops moved up to the front. The regulation horseshoe included holes for screwing in four crampons (*Hufeisen-Schraubstollen*). (© CIRIP, Alain Gesgon Collection)

On March 17, German forces in Bulgaria comprised 11½ divisions. As Prince Paul of Yugoslavia had proclaimed neutrality, his country was still a danger and, on March 25, he was obliged to submit to the Tripartite Pact. But during the night of March 26/27, the air force general, Simovic, seized power, put young Prince Peter II on the throne, let anti-German and pro-British demonstrations unfold, and then mobilized the country against the Third Reich. Faced with this treachery, on the 27th, with Order No. 25, Hitler decided to extend Operation *Marita*, the attack against Greece, to include all the Balkans in order to assist Italy. The next day, the great ally—Italy—suffered a decisive naval defeat at Cape Matapan at the hands of the Royal Navy.

On March 28, at 0400, the OKW sent a reworked *Marita* plan to the Italian General Staff via General von Rinteln, chief of the German liaison detachment. In this change of situation, the British saw an opportunity to create a coherent Balkan front including Yugoslavia and Greece, as well as Turkey, grouping together some 70 divisions facing the 30 or so lined up by the Germans. Another anti-German gesture was the signature of a friendship and non-aggression treaty between the Yugoslav government and the Soviets, which gave Hitler some comfort in terms of his intention to attack the USSR.

The launch of *Marita*, however, took everybody by surprise: on April 6, without any declaration of war, bombers from Luftflotte 4 under General Lohr bombed Belgrade, killing 17,000 civilians (*Unternehmen Strafgericht*—Operation *Chastisement*), and the 12th Army attacked in the region of the three frontiers, preceded by commando actions by II./Regiment Brandenburger, the Abwehr's special operations unit. (5, 7, and 8 companies wore the edelweiss on the jacket and the cap as the units were considered *Gebirgskompanien*. They also wore the color of the Jäger branch of arm (rifle green). The 6 had adopted the traditions of the cavalry hence the gold-yellow color of the arm.)

Breakthrough on the Metaxas Line

The British encouraged the Greeks to establish a defensive line situated much farther south, between Albania and north of Mount Olympus, along the bend in the Aliakmon. The Greeks preferred, however, to concentrate their effort backing onto the Metaxas Line, named after the late prime minister; this was a powerful, coherently fortified line, several miles deep, established along the northern frontier. This defensive system was there to ensure the routes providing access to the strategically important port of Thessalonica were covered. Building the line had taken six years. The highest fortress, the Rupesko, was 6,400 feet high, and the most powerful was the Istibei at 4,380 feet. In Greece, as in Yugoslavia, the terrain dominated: the valleys were the natural axes of penetration enclosed within very inaccessible mountains. The roads were narrow, running along the sides of escarpments.

With *Marita*, the German high command would take key points in depth, combining frontal attacks against all the Greek defenses using predominantly infantry in rapid breakthroughs or flanking maneuvers while employing armored and motorized units along the axes. The primary objective was Thessalonica, Greece's second town some 70 kilometers from the Bulgarian border, along the Vardar (the Yugoslav part) or Axios (Greek part) valley. This second mission was to be carried out by the 2. Panzerdivision, preceded by 8.(Geb)/Regt Brandenburg.

On April 5, XVIII. Gebirgskorps, under General Franz Böhme, massed along the border after moving up 370 miles by train and on foot through Bulgaria. Visual reconnoitering had been carried out by the HQs whose staff had sometimes worn Bulgarian dress as disguise. This permitted them to observe the Greeks continuing their work organizing defenses.

Orders for the attack were circulated. Each company knew what its objective was. Bombardment schedules for the artillery and the antitank guns were ready. The guns and ordnance had been hauled up by cable car and on muleback or even manually by night. The terrain was indeed abrupt and snow covered part of it, especially in 6.GD's area of operation.

Studying the map in the *Kompanietrupp*, the company squad. The men were issued the tapered *feldgrau* M40 trousers for the campaign. The officers are wearing tailormade *Bergmützen*. In the foreground, the arm of the company adjutant (Spiess) is visible with his two silver stripes. (© CIRIP, Alain Gesgon Collection)

Marching to the front.

The approach axes, which were visible to the Greek defenders from time to time, had to be cleared, especially at night; there were still frequent gusts of rain or snow, a very demanding situation for troops, animals, and vehicles.

A frontal attack on a coherent fortified line, in the mountains, defended by quality troops, was not the easiest of challenges. The Italians had experienced the same thing against the French in June 1940 when they had failed to break through the Alpine Maginot Line. Attempts to take the bridges situated behind the Metaxas Line, in the Struma valley, would likely fail too, given how impossible it was to penetrate the defense.

Indeed, if only three days were needed to drive the Greeks from their positions and advance on the axes leading to Thessalonica, it was primarily due to the outflanking maneuver executed by 2. Panzerdivision, advancing from Yugoslavia and attacking in pruning movements. The Greek forces in Thrace were now destabilized and effectively surrounded.

Faces are tense during a break. The stacked weapons are Gewehr 33/40 Mauser rifles, made in Bohemia-Moravia and issued from the beginning of the year to the mountain troops. Hot meals were still served from the field kitchens during the advance. (© CIRIP, Alain Gesgon Collection)

8cm mortar teams packing ordnance. The fuses have been placed in the shells. Although checked shirts were not regulation, they were often found in the mountain units. (© CIRIP, Alain Gesgon Collection)

Officers and NCOs prepare for their reconnaissance missions, first checking the staff maps. Dispatch riders are ready to transmit orders to the rest of the company. (© CIRIP, Alain Gesgon Collection)

This photograph is unique: it shows GJR100 officers and NCOs wearing Bulgarian uniform, including the company commander (bottom right) whom we have been following for several pages now. The group reconnoitered their axis of approach on the Metaxas Line wearing this dress. (© CIRIP, Alain Gesgon Collection)

In columns by section, on April 5, 1941, *Gebirgsjäger* headed for the border between Bulgaria and Greece. Behind the combat units came the baggage trains. (© CIRIP, Alain Gesgon Collection)

The Luftwaffe crossed the border during the night of April 5/6 to bomb Athens and Piraeus. The British merchant ship *Clan Fraser*, transporting 200 tons of explosives, blew up, destroying a good part of the port installations. Apart from a few *Jäger* wearing white camouflage dress in the snowed-over areas, the *Gebirgsjäger* and *Gebirgspioniere* in the first assault waves generally fought in simple combat dress, with only *Feldbluse*, so they would be comfortable, with an assault package limited to the contents of their shoulder bags, ammunition including the indispensable stick grenades, flamethrowers, explosive charges and *Zeltbahn* canvas ponchos which provided little protection against the cold and the icy gusts of rain that the combatants had to endure for three days running.

On April 6, 1941, at 0525, XVIII. Gebirgskorps opened the artillery barrage, and an hour later the assault detachments left their jump-off positions to infiltrate their objectives. They had been preceded by teams whose job it was to eliminate the advanced posts' "doorbells"—poisoning the guard dogs, etc.—and cut the Greek telephone lines. The battle of the borders had started. The fighting was particularly bitter. After 20 minutes of hammering hundreds of rounds per minute ahead of 5.GD, the Stukas dive-bombed the enemy fortifications, but their effect was limited if not useless.

Eventually, the advanced border posts fell, and subsequently the main strongholds were taken, the action stretching across XVIII.Geb.-AK's sector. On the east of the sector, the 72. Infanterie-Division under Major General Mattenklott came up in front of the Greek 14th and 7th Division strongpoints, particularly difficult where these joined. It succeeded in breaking through the first line of strongpoints but with heavy casualties, 700 killed and wounded.

At the junction between 72.ID and 5.GD—which had exchanged a battalion in order to ensure the "stitching" (*Naht*) between the two divisions held—was the Rupel defile, a natural obstacle where the Dinaric Alps, the Rhodope, and the Pinde meet. 5. and 6. Gebirgsdivisionen faced the Greek 18th Infantry Division, behind which the 19th Motorized Infantry Division was held in reserve to intercept any breakthrough. 5.GD made its initial push against the principal strongholds of Istibei, the "fortified mountain," flanked to the north by Kelkaïa, assigned respectively to GJR85 and 100.

During the night of April 6/7, it rained almost non-stop, coupled with constant artillery fire being exchanged between the German and Greek positions. Columns of men hauled ammunition, ordnance, and explosives up to the frontlines, as well as jerrycans of fuel and other resupplies.

It took the division three days to break through the fortified line, alternating with capturing strongpoints and simultaneously infiltrating the lines to attack the next ones. It was the baptism of fire for this young division and the attackers learned more on the first day than in all the months of peacetime training, Indeed, every type of divisional weapon and tactic was used including demolition charges, smoke-bombs, flamethrowers, jerrycans of fuel thrown into air vents, antitank guns and flak guns dragged to the strongpoints themselves with great difficulty, or firing from the opposite slopes (using the 8.8cm guns for embrasure fire as against the Maginot Line), and hand-to-hand fighting against the Evzones, elite Greek troops stationed between strongpoints. II./GJR85 was ordered to break through up to the valley of the Struma and Neon Patritsi, a natural fault along which also ran the Thessalonica–Seres–Drama railway line. The terrible weather and continuous rain made discreet movement easier.

The surrender of enemy forces in Thrace on April 9 at 0900 enabled the Germans to resume their advance, though some units were still blocked. Indeed 2. Panzerdivision, which had left Bulgaria to take Strumica in Yugoslavia, had broken across the border into Greece, along the Vardar and had reached Thessalonica by overwhelming the Greek reserve units. This was made possible by the action of 8.(Geb.)/Brandenburg who, wearing Yugoslav uniforms, had succeeded in capturing the two bridges over the Vardar—Gallikos and then Axiopoulos—before the British or the Greeks were able to destroy them. First Lieutenant Grabert was awarded the Knight's Cross. Certain strongpoints like the Popotlivitsa and the Rupesko only surrendered several hours after the ceasefire and they too had to be taken

Photographs taken during the fighting are rare. The gunners here are having trouble getting their 7.5cm mountain gun into battery on the upward slope, in the afternoon of April 5. (Aquarelle by Hans Liska)

On April 6, 1941, the first elements in contact with the enemy, *Jäger* or *Pioniere*, wore light dress, their mission being to cut barbed-wire. Getting through these obstacles was vital so that the concrete strongpoints could be approached discreetly. Very few combatants attacked wearing white snow dress, usually made locally. During the three days' offensive, the only protection was from the *Zeltbahn*.

after heavy fighting. At the end of 40 hours of fighting, 5.GD was able to advance along the Struma valley unimpeded. Its losses were high: 155 killed, five missing and 457 wounded, almost an entire battalion.

As for 6. Gebirgsdivision, it was formed in Romania between February 12–29 and transported in 79 trains. On March 2, it entered Bulgaria which it traversed from north to south—267 miles—in 12 days. Leaving its deployment zone at Petric, it attacked on the morning of April 6 along the western axis of XVIII.Geb.-AK, toward the southwest after a night's waiting in the snow, with the light supply columns to the rear, ready to follow.

The assault detachments of the vanguard units wearing light dress and carrying no equipment, dealt with the border posts with pistols and grenades. The *Jäger* companies followed immediately.

Gebirgspioniere attacking a Greek position with a flamethrower.

Despite several Greek counterattacks and accurate artillery fire from Mount Krusia, the Germans reached the key zone of the Belacitsa chain. The commander of GJR141, Colonel Eberling, was killed by a bullet in the head standing next to Schörner who was once again in the vanguard.

By the evening of April 6, the objective for the day had been achieved. But the need to align with other units meant they had to mark time on the 7th. The next day, however, the division was able to make use of a breach half a mile wide in the enemy lines, discovered by a patrol during the night, to discover that the strongpoints had not been totally achieved. It was only on April 8 at 1600 and without the planned Stuka attack because of the terrible weather, that 6.GD was able to start attacking the second line of strongpoints, those on Mount Krusia.

At 1900 a breakthrough was made to the west, across almost open terrain, on either side of the hamlet of Anatoli. The Greeks ran away, abandoning all their equipment. A German company then took a regiment of 2,000 men by surprise in a wood. After a few mortar shots and an assault on foot, the Greeks surrendered.

What had seemed impossible had been successfully carried out in three days by lightly armed troops from these two mountain divisions: firstly a breakthrough in a strongly fortified zone some 3,250 yards deep, high up in the mountains and at the end of winter, before pursuing the enemy through a forced march to take him from behind. This succession of quick actions, together with the panzer breakthrough near Thessalonica, destabilized the whole of the Thracian front. 6.GD had reached its second *Angriffsziel* (attack objective), the Akrolimnion–Krusia–Oros Heights southwest of Iraklion, 18½ miles inside the border.

But 5. and 6.GDen were on foot, facing enemy units that were cut off and therefore unaware of the surrender. So, on the 10th, the motorized offensive was able to continue for the next phase: to drive a wedge between the Yugoslavs to the west and the Greeks and British to the east, to prevent any coordinated action by the Allies. A 2. Panzer-division *Kampfgruppe* succeeded in breaking through toward Larissa, east of Mount Olympus, by using the coastal roads and the Tempi Gorges, down which flowed the Pinios; their

Infantry and *Pioniere* attack a Greek strongpoint with explosives.

objective was to take the New Zealanders from the rear, between Mount Olympus (5,950 feet) and the Pinde chain. 6.GD was given the job of reducing enemy pressure by creating a diversion by outflanking the enemy from the west, over the mountain with the western Tempi Gorges as the objective.

The reinforced 2.GJR/143 departed to reconnoiter in the morning of the 16th, followed in the afternoon by III. and II./GJR143 which had left the main axis at Leptohkaria. I/GJR143 caught up in the morning of the 17th. Then it was GAR118 and GJR141. The heavily laden units left on foot, with mules bearing the heavy weapons, and the baggage trains remaining on the main road. Supplies were brought in by Junkers Ju 52/3ms, which dropped food and forage.

The weather was initially warm and dry but this changed to icy rain before settling down again shortly before the attack, carried out all day on the 18th, against the New Zealanders and Australians set up in and around the villages of Evangelismos, Parapotamos, and Gonos so as to control the Pinios River. The fighting was costly with GJR143 suffering 13 killed and 70 wounded. Against well-set up positions, the terrain offered few opportunities for advancing safely. The wounded Germans and New Zealanders left behind during the withdrawal were attended to that evening.

On the morning of the 19th, 2/GJR143, still the vanguard along the main axis, joined up with advanced elements of 2. Panzerdivision at Larissa where it managed to capture a large stock of supplies. The same day, the division was able to benefit from a one-day pause, very welcome after 13 days' almost uninterrupted pursuit. Schörner had indeed advanced at the same time, at the head of the rest of his division toward Gianitsa, in a motorized vanguard made up around Aufklärungs-Abteilung 112 using captured vehicles. On April 19, the *Vorausabteilung* from 6.GD took part in the capture of Larissa alongside 2. Panzerdivision.

An aquarelle taken from the *Landser*, a "*Groschen-Heft*," a penny-press newspaper which was published after the war, in an issue devoted to the attack against the Metaxas Line. (DR)

Gebirgsjäger and *Gebirgspioniere* gathered at the entrance of the Kelkaïa strongpoint after its capture. (DR)

Once the first strongpoints were overwhelmed, *Gebirgsjäger* assembled their Greek prisoners. Troops between strongpoints were Evzones, light mountain infantry who were particularly combative. After the first line of defense was subdued, General Schörner issued orders for the capture of the second. The vegetation has changed, and the snow has almost disappeared. (DR)

Major General Schörner advances with his motorized vanguard which linked up with 2. Panzerdivision armored columns.

The obstacles along the Axios and the parallel roads had not really slowed down the German advance. A patrol from 6.GD had hoisted the Reich flag on Mount Olympus on April 16 during a memorable snowstorm. In the end, the whole of XVIII.Geb.-AK, with the support of a commando from 8.(Geb.)/Brandenburg wearing British uniforms, had crossed the Aliakmon and surrounded the Mount Olympus massif.

On the 19th, the Greek prime minister committed suicide. Schörner took advantage of the rest to circulate among his soldiers, congratulating his companies. The following day he was awarded the Knight's Cross. On April 21, at Larissa, Greek plenipotentiaries signed the unconditional capitulation of their country.

A single obstacle still blocked the Germans' way, the Thermopylae Pass, the Greek capital's traditional defense. The New Zealand 2nd Infantry Division (General Freyberg), with two brigades and some Greek elements refused to capitulate, and, acting as rearguard, tried to cover the Allied withdrawal. It only managed to hold out against the 6.GD *Kampfgruppe* and 5. Panzerdivision for one day, the 24th, inflicting nonetheless heavy losses on the German forces. The bulk of the Commonwealth expeditionary force, harassed by the Luftwaffe, managed to embark 50,000 men for Crete on April 26, since German progress was slowed down by the rearguard in the Thebes region and because the bridges across the Corinth Canal had been destroyed. On April 27, the German flag was hoisted on the Acropolis in Athens and Schörner was appointed military commandant of the city.

Here again the Brandenburgers (from 8.(Geb.)-Kp) had been sent ahead to secure the key bridges around Athens, alongside the *Fallschirmjäger* who had tried unsuccessfully to capture intact the bridge across the Corinth Canal. On April 30, the whole of Greece was in the hands of the Germans, Italians, and Bulgarians. On May 3, a victory parade was organized in the capital with 6.GD at its head.

During this period 5.GD had resumed its march southward, on foot of course, in the second echelon. Before reaching Athens, it was given preparatory orders relating to *Unternehmen Merkur*—Operation *Mercury*, the conquest of Crete.

Thermopylae Pass was captured by 6.GD on April 24. Note the Dunlop-sponsored bilingual sign indicating the site.

XXXXIX. Gebirgs-Armeekorps in Yugoslavia

Still in the context of *Marita*, Yugoslavia was attacked on the same day as was Greece and its Metaxas Line, along two major axes. Stationed at Wolfsberg, between Klagenfuhrt and Graz in Austria, XXXXIX.Geb.-AK (Lieutenant General Ludwig Kübler), under the 2nd Army (Colonel General von Weichs), appeared with 1.GD on the border between the Ostmark (annexed Austria) and Yugoslavia on April 8 along a secondary axis, the southernmost point of the attack dispositions. Although the panzers had to rush toward the capital, Belgrade, the 2nd Army's objective was Sarajevo via Zagreb (Agram). But 2nd Army's preparation for *Marita* looked like a vast improvisation, as units were starting to move north for *Barbarossa*, in regions with inadequate rail and road networks.

On their side the Yugoslav troops were not ready; their arms were out of date and not adapted to a modern war. Cohesion was also a problem among diverse populations with ethnic, cultural, and religious tensions. Some Yugoslavs actually laid down their arms still in their storage grease, without having fired a single shot.

Successive truckloads of German troops were assembled between April 5–8 in terrible weather with only limited baggage trains and communications, before a serious outbreak of grippe (flu) struck down hundreds. In a region inadequately equipped with billets, 1.GD, under the command of General Hubert Lanz and reinforced by *Landesschützen* from Klagenfuhrt, crossed the border between Bleiburg and Lavamünd; its initial objective was to break through the fortified Yugoslav positions to the east of the Kamniske-Savinjske (Steiner Alps) between Prevalje (Pollein) and Dravograd (Unterdrauburg), centered on Ravne na Koroskem (Gutenstein), then capture Slovenj Gradec (Windisch-Graz) and break through to Celje (Cilli) along two axes.

Reconnaissance beyond the border started on April 6, the opening of the offensive against the Metaxas Line. Initial reports allowed the Germans to believe that the Ravne na Koroskem (Gutenstein) fortifications would not offer much resistance. On the 8th, the *Landesschützen* crossed the border at Dolga Brda and Lavamünd.

They then moved along the northern bank of the Meza (Mischbach) to provide 1.GD with an axis of advance. The bulk of

On April 27, something of a *Hetzjagd* (a "fox hunt") drove several mountain units forward. It was finally a motorized element of 8.(Geb.)/Brandenburg under the command of Captain Jacobi, the battalion commander, that raised the *Reichskriegsflagge* on the Acropolis, marking the taking of the Greek capital. (Colorized document)

the division was still on the way, between Salzburg and Vienna, hoping to arrive in time for the offensive. Along the western axis, scouts managed to flank the fortifications whereas GJR99 (Colonel Hermann Kress), reinforced and based on three sub-groups, crossed the Meza, came into contact with the enemy, captured the strongpoints around Ravne na Koroskem (Gutenstein), and took control of the heights to the south of the river.

On the eastern axis, during the night of the April 8/9, *Pioniere*, supported by *Panzerjäger*, crossed the Drave on inflatable dinghies and set up a bridgehead at Dravograd (Unter-Drauburg), as the road and rail bridges had been destroyed by the Yugoslavs. Vorausabteilung Lang (once again based on Geb.-Panzerjäger-Abteilung 44 commanded by Lieutenant Colonel Lang), reinforced with *Pioniere*, climbed the southern bank, moved out of the bridgehead and attacked the fortifications on the southern heights of the river. In order to set up the junction with Lang, Kress had the *Panzerjäger-Kp* from GJR99 intervene, reinforced by a howitzer used in direct firing. The Yugoslavs made good use of their concrete fortifications and their frontline troops but during the evening of the 9th, they started to fall back southward. The bulk of the division progressively caught up the *Kampfgruppen* by the end of the day

On April 10, after a very uncomfortable night, the advance resumed westward by Crna na Koroskem (Schwarzenbach), the Sleme Pass (St Vid), the valley of Velenje (Schönstein), and Zalec (Smarino) in the valley of the Sanija (Sann); and on the eastern axis, along the valley of the Mislinja, by Slovenj Gradec (Windisch-Graz)—the wrecked railway tunnel there temporarily slowed down the advance—and Vojnik (Hohenegg). As soon as resistance was encountered, the leading units dealt with it while support echelons deployed up hill and down dale, dragging their antitank guns by hand. Daytime and nighttime ambushes caused significant casualties for 1.GD. Yugoslav resistance indeed was stiffening. On the 11th, a textbook German divisional attack was mounted in the direction of Celje (Cilli) via Vojnik. But the enemy had disappeared, so the reinforced Vorausabteilung Lang, with General Lanz in the second lead vehicle—the first was a 2cm FlaK gun—entered Celje. The population, mainly *Volkdeutsche*—"outside Germans"— excitedly welcomed 1.GD.

A detachment of 5.GD, likely from GJR100, after the fighting in Thrace, was sent to Thessalonica where they took in the sights. The Rotunda of Saint-George's church is visible. (© CIRIP, Alain Gesgon Collection)

Gruppe Kress, moving down the valley of the Savinja (Sann) along two axes, reached Celje by reconnoitering southward. The commander of III./GJR99, Major Hörl, was appointed *Stadtkommandant* (town commandant) of Celje. During the evening of April 11, leaving part of the division to rest and finish reorganizing, Lang resumed his advance on Zagreb (Agram), reinforced by *Jäger* in trucks and by Flak, via Laško (Tüffer).

The impression was that the enemy had started to scatter: isolated, unarmed soldiers were returning home. PoW camps were hastily improvised along the route, village mayors being given the task of housing and feeding the captured soldiers. With Zagreb, the Croat capital, now the objective, liaison was established with the panzers of 14. Panzerdivision coming from Barcs (Barcz), 125 miles directly east. At Metlika, the *Vorausabteilung* split in two, one part proceeding to Zagreb where 1.GD with two infantry divisions relieved 14. Panzerdivision which continued its advance. The other half continued toward Krka (Gurk), via Mokronog (Mirna) and Novo Mesto (Rudolfswerth), then to Kupa (Kulpa) via Metlika, in order to form a bridgehead on April 12, enabling the bulk of the division to take Karlovac (Karlstadt) the next day. Lang accomplished his mission without encountering any serious resistance from the rearguards. The division had penetrated 62 miles of enemy territory, but much of it was spread out along the route, with GRJ98 still being disembarked at Wiener-Neustadt.

On the 12th, ahead of 14. Panzerdivision heading toward Zagreb (Agram), was a section of 5.(Geb.)/Brandenburg which left Celje (Cilli) for Karlovac (Karlstadt), passing the 2nd Army en route. From there, it made contact with the Italians, via Stupicka and Delnice, at Fiume on the shores of the Adriatic.

The Yugoslav high command appeared not to want to contest the invasion along the Kupa, but rather withdraw a maximum of troops southward to save them from being

Units in Yugoslavia advanced as far as possible along the axes, like this PaK 36 towed by a *Krupp-Protze*—which is not in the advance echelon as the gun is still covered with a tarpaulin.

Yugoslav prisoners being disarmed by a 1.GD PaK 36 unit. Shell boxes are visible on the ground. (DR)

captured. Lanz therefore decided to pursue the enemy with 1.GD keeping in constant contact. On April 13, the division occupied Karlova (Karlstadt) without a fight. The population asked for protection from the Italians advancing from the west (Delnice). 1.GD continued toward Bihac where advance units from 14. Panzerdivision were starting to arrive. Bosnia was a Muslim society unfamiliar to the Bavarians with its minarets, chadors, and men wearing fezzes.

On the 14th, elements from 1.GD at Karlovac and Bihac watched as elements of 14. Panzerdivision, which made up the right wing of XXXXVI. AK(mot.) of the 2nd Army, overtook it, exploiting the situation in the direction of Donji Vakuf and Sarajevo. But the order to fall back on Celje reached the division during the morning of April 15 as the *Jäger* were starting to dream of entering Sarajevo. Meanwhile, on the 11th, Croatia declared its independence; on the 13th, Belgrade fell; and on the 14th, Sarajevo was occupied. On April 17, the ceasefire was signed and 350,000 Yugoslav prisoners were marched into captivity.

After celebrating the victory at Celje (Cilli) with the *Volksdeutschen*, the division started on its way back to the Reich. It settled around the Wörher See,

4.GD reaches the Belgrade area. An HQ staff officer has arrived in a civilian car. His rucksack is on the mudguard. (© CIRIP, Alain Gesgon Collection)

between Pörtschach and Klagenfurt. A part of 1.GD was already moving towards Poland via Slovakia when Hitler visited the division—which he called the *Garde-Division* (from the Prussian Imperial Guard)—at Klagenfurt. Finally, the division reached its position in the line, in Galicia on the border with Russia. For XXXXIX.Geb.-AK, the Yugoslav interlude was over.

4. Gebirgsdivision as a part of XIV. Panzerkorps in Yugoslavia

Another division that took part in the Yugoslav campaign was 4.GD (under Major General Karl Eglseer), within XIV. Armeekorps (mot.)/Panzergruppe 1 (von Kleist) of List's 12th Army. It reached Bulgaria (in the Sofia area) via Hungary and Romania to experience its baptism of fire, in the natural fortresses of the mountainous regions. On April 8, at 0530, lead units of 11. Panzerdivision of XIV.AK (mot.) crossed the border at Brodec, through the frontier pass at Arabakonak toward Niš—an important crossroads in Serbia, alongside a railway line, on a tributary of the Morava—via Pirot.

4.GD succeeded in following 11. Panzerdivision up to Pirot, on isolated terrain, with muddy secondary roads because of the very wet weather, and facing an elusive adversary. However, the lead elements of the mountain division were motorized, ready to react immediately, but were interlocked with those of the armored division. Therefore, the *Gebirgsjäger*, on foot often had to march off-road, in the mire and the half-melted snow, leaving the roads for the vehicles.

Apart from the tortuous, slippery main roads, the hamlets and villages were served only by a network of tracks. Nevertheless, Pirot was captured after a brief exchange of fire.

After the fighting in the Bihac region, XXXXIX.Geb.-AK has a well-earned rest, with priority given to food, but also in keeping administrative documents—*Leitz* files, still used today in the German administration—and war diaries up to date (© CIRIP, Alain Gesgon Collection)

1.GD rests in the Bihac region. The *Jäger* sitting front right, is wearing a captured British shirt with sports trousers. The bare-chested *Jäger* in front is wearing climbing shoes. (DR)

The first panzers entered Niš in the morning of April 9; the valley of the Morava and the major north–south railway was "*in deutscher Hand*." The Yugoslavs counterattacked but could not retake lost ground: the road to Belgrade was open. The prisoners lined up in the thousands, and were soon put to work filling in shell craters, alongside the mountains of matériel either destroyed or captured. In the evening on the 9th, the armored vanguard took Kragujevac on the main axis toward Belgrade, along the Velika Morava toward Aleksina, Cupriia, and Jagodina.

Although 4.GD was not directly involved here, Kragujevac has to be mentioned as it was where the national arsenal produced weapons for the Yugoslav army. Seeing the Germans arriving, the manager of the arsenal had weapons distributed to personnel who turned into snipers—*Heckenschützen* or "free shooters," hated by the Germans because they did not wear identifiable uniforms—who were the forerunners of Josip Broz Tito's resistance movement that was to cause such heavy losses for the occupiers, and such atrocious German reprisals among the population until the end of 1944.

At Pirot, on April 11, the *Gebirgsjäger* moved off to the northeast, along the border, to cover the corps to the north. They took Knjaževac then continued northward and eastward, launching reconnaissance missions along several axes. It was thus that a Lieutenant Schotters, possibly a Brandenburger, in a halftrack so as not to waste time, was reconnoitering several bridges toward the village of Boljevac, when, in the village of Dubropoltje, he managed to capture the enemy's divisional commander and eight senior officers. The prize was brought back to the divisional HQ at Knjaževac for questioning. The next day (Easter Sunday), Schotters was awarded the Iron Cross 1st and 2nd Class by the divisional commander. He later, on the same day, rescued a Flak battery that had been ambushed and managed to capture further prisoners and some documents of interest.

Moving up and down the terrain was exhausting. The "*Mulis*" proved indispensable, since the *Jäger* themselves carried only the bare minimum; gasmasks, for instance, were attached to the saddles of the pack mules. Each daily stage, including patrols dealing with incidents, was between 25 and 30 miles in length.

Over the next two days, two Yugoslav divisions surrendered and the northeastern region of Niš was cleared. Along the western axis, moving on from Knjaževac, the *Gebirgsjäger* captured Knjaževac, at the junction of the Zapadna Morava and the Rasina rivers, after crossing the Juzna Morava. Resistance was weak, losses light, and PoWs were numerous.

Following the ceasefire on April 18, 4.GD remained as the occupying force in the Belgrade region, taken by 11. Panzerdivision on the 13th—jointly with 2. SS-Panzerdivision Das Reich coming down from the north—before joining up with those units preparing for Operation *Barbarossa*.

Crete

Entrusted to XI. Fliegerkorps under General der Flieger Kurt Student for the land component, Hitler decided on the conquest of Crete on April 20, presented in directive No. 25 on the 25th. The aim was to finish off the Balkan campaign, particularly successful up until then, and to prepare for control of the Eastern Mediterranean basin.

Having a natural springboard within striking distance of Egypt with a view to supporting the North Africa campaign, which itself aimed at conquering the region at least up to the Nile Delta, was not apparently instrumental in the Führer's decision. For Operation *Merkur*, 22. Luftlande-Division (airmobile division) was replaced by 5.GD, reinforced by a regiment from 6.GD in the process of being reorganized after operations in the north of Greece.

Planning included transporting the *Gebirgstruppen* in two waves, as early as the second day, by air using the airfields seized by the parachutists; the second by sea with the heavy matériel, including a battalion of tanks. The objective was to enlarge the "oil drops" (the captured sites) all at the same time, and then getting them to gradually join up. But planning underestimated several key facts: the narrowness of the sites chosen for the drops, the lack of roads (one single major road along the north of the island), the lack of means for tactical radio transmission, only one reasonable-sized port (Souda Bay), 40,000 British and Commonwealth troops (not 15,000), and a Cretan population infinitely more hostile than that on continental Greece.

Because they were able to decipher communications sent by Enigma, the British were well informed of the major elements of the imminent attack. Finally, the parachuting methods of the time meant that the men—who once on

These *Gebirgsjäger* don't seem overly worried by the prospect of a flight in a Ju 52 to their new operational theater: Crete.

The "*Kreta*" armband was the second commemorative armband introduced during the war. Considered as a *Kampfabzeichen* (combat insignia), it was adopted on October 18, 1942 for the Heer. It was introduced gradually, since the model had not been decided upon earlier. This example was worn by Captain Pröhl of GJR100.

Although no color photograph taken in a "*kleine Schiffstaffel*" (small squadron) has ever been found, this "*Ullr*" from 13./GJR100, was one of the first to appear in the war. The regiment lost a whole battalion, sunk with all hands by the Royal Navy. The "*Ullr*," the medal of Saint Ulrich, the patron saint of winter sports, appeared throughout the war with a theme for each operation.

the ground sometimes had only a pistol—and their equipment in containers including their weapons, were dropped separately; this method was to cause heavy casualties among the *Fallschirmerjäger*. One could add that the uniforms and equipment were those for the campaign in northern Greece, very different conditions from the scorching Cretan spring. The decision to not equip the troops with tropical uniforms was taken so as not to compromise the operation.

At dawn on May 20 (Ascension Day[1]), leaving relatively little time for the Allies to recover, the first wave jumped into Crete. By evening, not all the objectives had been achieved but the British defense had not reacted. As the operations against Rethimnon and Heraklion were relative failures, the effort switched to Maleme.

On May 21, the second wave (FJR1 and 2) jumped or arrived by sea (5.GD in the afternoon). The group "*Ost*" (east) under the command of General Ringel had to attack the town of Heraklion and its aerodrome. Under his command was placed for this operation what he called a "*Luftlandemarinegebirgsdivision*" (air- and seaborne mountain division) made up of its three mountain regiments with three battalions each, its artillery regiment with four groups, as well as its organic units, together with the paratroopers already deployed. Two groups were made up in order to transport all these units (II. and III./GJR85 as well as III./GJR100), heavy and logistics equipment included. The first of two "light flotillas" was made up of 60 or so civilian boats of all types and sizes, including fishing vessels. A number

1 "Ascension" was *"(Christi-)Himmelfahrt"* in German; a *"Himmelsfahrtkommando,"* or an "Ascension Commando" denoted a high-risk mission, sometimes also called *"Ritterkreuz Unternehmen"* (Knight's Cross operation).

Once on the ground, *Gebirgsjäger* deployed to assist the paratroopers, like these machine-gunners in a vineyard behind a dry-stone wall, and the Junkers Ju 52 which has landed them. The *feldgrau* uniform was maintained to mask the operation even though tropical uniforms had already existed in the Afrikakorps since early 1941. (DR)

The "savior" of *Unternehmen Merkur* was without doubt Major General Julius Ringel, commander of the reinforced 5.GD. Without the (planned) intervention of his troops, the parachute troops by themselves would have been defeated. An Austrian, nicknamed "Papa" Ringel, he was particularly appreciated by his subordinates. The battle for Crete earned him the Knight's Cross. (Colorized document, DR)

This colorized photo shows us that not only troops suffer in the heatwave. This *Obergefreiter*, wearing a pair of English shorts, is looking after the village donkey, giving it water in a Tommy's helmet. (DR)

The heavy cloth dress rapidly proved unsuitable for conditions and British army shorts quickly replaced the *Berghosen*, giving a typical "Kreta" look to these *Gebirgsjäger* advancing to Souda Bay.

of them, often small vessels for inshore fishing and unsuited to the 186-mile crossing, broke down or were sunk by the Royal Navy between Milos and Crete (shooting and ramming) causing 400 men to drown, almost all of III./GJR100.

Security at sea depended on only two Italian destroyers which revealed the improvised or even rash nature of the enterprise. During the day the Luftwaffe, however, intervened with its Stukas which caused the British heavy casualties and relieved the *Gebirgsjäger*'s crossing. The second group, making up the third wave in fact, with the rest of 5.GD, arrived by Ju 52s and gliders, using the aerodromes captured by the paratroopers. Maleme was but a small aerodrome, handkerchief-sized, 495 by 165 yards, which the *Jäger* discovered littered with wrecked Ju 52s that the British were still shooting at. Once again Ringel had come up against one of the Germans' adversaries in Greece, Freyberg.

5.GD *Gebirgsjäger* began consolidating the bridgehead at Maleme by taking the surrounding heights. Then, after making up their strength on the 22nd, on May 24, they began their offensive on the north coast, along the only road suitable for vehicles, with attacks to the west then inland, and at times as far as the south coast over mountainous terrain. The hardest fighting was for Galatas, less than six miles from Canea, on the 25th and 26th. After

Gebirgsjäger pay tribute to a comrade. The makeshift grave is covered with a *Fliegertuch* (air-to-ground identification panel).

two days of stubborn resistance, with alternating attacks and counterattacks, the Allied division broke off in front of Kampfgruppe Utz (commander of GJR100) and Ramcke's *Fallschirmjäger*, leaving the road open to Canea. At the same time, during the night of May 24/25, Kampfgruppe Krakau (commander of GJR85) began penetrating the mountainous south, the Kochrana and Achladedi Hills not overly high but comprising exceedingly difficult terrain.

On the 25th and 26th, GJR141 from 6.GD (Colonel Jais) arrived on the island by air to reinforce 5.GD. It was engaged the following morning between GJR85 and GJR100 to outflank Canea and took part in the action to take Souda Bay, the only port able to take the large Kriegsmarine vessels.

I./GJR141 ran up against resistance a few miles east of Maleme, near the chapel, three-quarters of a mile east of the Pyrgos Bridge. Resuming its advance, with the *Rgt.-Stab* and III./GJR141 following, the battalion again met resistance at Katsifarina at the southeastern exits of Canea. During the morning, the battalion resumed its progress toward Souda Bay but an enemy counterattack caused a breakdown in communications among regimental orderly officers and dispatch riders. The commander of I./GJR141 finally managed to contact the *Stab* and reported that his company had run up against resistance in a thick olive grove and had suffered heavy losses from mines, forcing him to return to Katsifarina. The battalion's casualty tally was 215, including nine officers (three of whom were company commanders), and 122 other ranks killed.

On May 27, the New Zealand resistance around Stilos to the southeast of the island's capital was reduced by Kampfgruppe Krakau which took the Kalami Bridge before it could be destroyed, enabling the tempo of the pursuit toward Heraklion to be maintained. Kampfgruppe Wittmann (commander of GAR95) got the advance going again toward Rhetimnon and Heraklion. The *Gebirgsjäger* were thus able to gradually relieve the *Fallschirmjäger*, especially those in the third assault wave torn to pieces at Heraklion (FJR2), their assigned objective for *Merkur*.

On May 28, Allied troops started evacuating to Egypt, but by focusing on the Allies falling back to the east of the island, the Germans overlooked units which were exfiltrating to the south, at the fishing port of Sfakia. I. and II./GJR100 from Kampfgruppe Utz, began pursuing them in vain until the next day, hindered by rearguard action, in particular to

Gebirgsjäger observe the results of a Stuka and artillery bombardment. This image, no doubt colorized at the time, shows some interesting details, like the binoculars, the informal dress of the *Jäger* in the center, the "captured" shorts, and the *Fliegertuch*. (Private collection)

"Papa" Ringel presenting decorations to his *Jäger* after the fighting. Rolled-up British shorts were *de rigueur.*

the north of Kare and the Imbro Pass. On the evening of May 30, Crete was "*in deutscher Hand*" and *Merkur* was closed on June 1.

The fighting was hard because the Allies, even if they had difficulty coordinating their operations through poor leadership, defended bitterly. Moreover, the 46°C temperatures were debilitating for the *Jäger* in their woolen uniforms; they quickly got hold of captured British gear, especially shorts. In the end, 5.GD had without any doubt saved the operation; Crete had become the "paratroopers' graveyard" (General Student). Facing 60,000 British, Australian, and New Zealand troops, the mountain troops had captured 15,000 enemy soldiers and 300 guns. In all *Merkur* had cost the Germans 5,000 casualties, of which 1,150 were from 5.GD.

5.GD remained on the island as the occupying force for six months then left in December for Karelia. The *Gebirgsjäger* maintained good relations with the local population, notably during the harvest in which they took part. Ringel was made an honorary citizen of Heraklion and a plaza still bears his name. However, local resistance soon sprang up, assisted in no small part by the rugged terrain, ideal for guerrilla warfare.

Relaxation was the order of the day in 5.GD (GJR100) after the fighting. This off-duty officer suntans in a captured vehicle, amidst British webbing and a pith helmet. (© CIRIP, Alain Gesgon Collection)

The Eastern Front, 1941–42

The previous chapter described mountain unit operations during the Balkan interlude that delayed the start of the invasion of the USSR, Operation *Barbarossa*. On April 10, 1941, Stalin put his western districts on alert and, on May 6, he was appointed head of the government and Commander-in-Chief of the Red Army.

Underestimating the extent of Soviet territory, its climate, the strength of the Red Armed forces—and so the lessons that should have been learned from history—and fearing that Stalin might attack the Reich, or at least join the Allied camp, Hitler decided to wage, as he saw it, a preventive war against the USSR, thus violating the Molotov–Ribbentrop Pact signed in 1939. From early 1941 the vanguards of three army groups (*Heeresgruppen*) began deploying from East Prussia to Romania: *Süd* (South) von Rundstedt, *Mitte* (Center) von Bock, and *Nord* (North) von Leeb. Initially, the mountain divisions would only fight within Army Group South and simultaneously on the Finnish front (see following chapter).

Some divisions joined later Army Group North at the beginning of 1942, brought into position by rail to their jump-off points near the demarcation lines set up by the Soviets. The order for the attack—"*Dortmund*"—was given during the night of June 20/21.

Without wearing their *Blechhut*—their tin hats, or *Stahlhelm* (steel helmet)—because of the June heat, these 1.GD machine-gunners support their company advance in a cotton field. (Franz Moll Archives)

The *Gebirgsartilleristen* followed right behind the attacking troops. (1.GD Association)

Army Group South

XXXXIX.Geb.-AK (Lieutenant General Ludwig Kübler), under the command of the 17th Army (von Stülpnagel) and Army Group South, at the southern tip of the offensive line, broke through with 1.GD and 68.ID in the advance echelon on Sunday, June 22, 1941 at dawn (0320). 4.GD, initially in the OKH reserve, followed. The opening artillery barrage did not prevent heavy fighting as soon as Kübler breached the Germano-Soviet border into occupied Poland, in spite of the element of surprise in the initial hours.

During the early days of *Barbarossa*, XXXXIX.Geb.-AK *Gebirgsjäger* captured thousands of prisoners, guarded here by *Jäger* and Flak personnel. (Franz Moll Archives)

On June 25 there occurred a surprise which proved strategic: the appearance on the battlefield of one of the best tanks of the war, the T-34. German initiative and courage made up for the technological handicap, and several tanks were destroyed by the mountain units.

GJR99 (Colonel Kress) of 1.GD met immediate resistance, but managed to take the fortified Hill 273 on the first day. GJR98 (Colonel Picker) took Oleszycec. The Soviet response was not long in coming as Red Army infantry and artillery—97th Fusiliers and Frontier Guards, from Siberia—met the invaders. Divisional commander, Major General Hubert Lanz, was himself slightly wounded in his HQ post at Judengraben. That day was,

III./GAR79 horse-drawn batteries, equipped with the 10.5cm FH18, needed to deploy rapidly across the battlefield. (Franz Moll Archives)

In Profile:
General Ludwig Kübler
September 2, 1889–August 18, 1947

Kübler joined the Bavarian Army in 1908 and saw action in the Great War, being awarded the Iron Cross 1st and 2nd Class. After the war he was retained in the Reichswehr. In 1938 he assumed command of the 1st Mountain Division (1.GD). He was involved in the Polish campaign, as well as the invasion of the Low Countries and France. In April 1941, Kübler's XXXXIX Mountain Corps participated in the Balkan campaign, before seeing action during Operation *Barbarossa*. After two years as commander of the 4th Army on the Eastern Front, he returned to the Balkans in October 1943. As commander of LXXXXVII Army Corps in early 1945, he was captured by Yugoslav partisans, tried for war crimes, and hanged in 1947.

Disfigured on the left side of his face by a war wound sustained in the Great War, Kübler always tended to face left when having his photo taken. (Zygmunt Wasilewski)

Lanz (left) and Kübler preparing for the second battle of Lemberg. These two generals, who did not see eye to eye, are wearing camouflage covers for their *Schulterstücken* (shoulder boards), as a symbol of command from the front. The insignias of the *Bergmütze* are woven in silver and the buttons are gold. Kübler has added a metal cockade to his. (Franz Moll Archives)

according to the 1.GD *Kriegstagebuch* (war diary), the hardest and bloodiest that the division had encountered to date (18 officers lost), in particular during the capture of the castle at Oleszyce. By the first evening, 1.GD had advanced eight miles.

On the 23rd and 24th, GJR98 advanced without great difficulty, whereas GJR99 had trouble taking enemy positions under heavy artillery fire. Taking Hill 235 by the Fleischmann Battalion cost the lives of four out of five company commanders. On June 25, 1.GD was faced with a surprise: tanks from the 3rd Soviet Armored Corps attacked its lead elements. They were taken to task by GJR98's PaK 37s but the shells ricocheted off the armor: the first T-34s had just appeared on the battlefield.

On his own initiative, *Jäger* Berauer, from 13./GJR98, a skiing champion, climbed up onto one of these steel monsters and threw grenades down the gun barrel. Others quickly imitated him and the attack was stopped in this way. But the regiments no longer had confidence in their antitank guns—Geb.PJA44 was partly equipped with more efficient 5cm PaK M38s.

Over the following days, breakthroughs, ambushes, and armored counterattacks were the order of the day, the enemy appearing to fall back in good order toward the Dniester River, with strong rearguards to slow the Germans. 1.GD, supported by Sturmgeschütze, advanced along the same route they had taken in 1939, toward Lemberg, in front of which they stopped on June 30.

On the 26th, 4.GD (Major General von Eglseer) relieved 68.ID, which had been torn to pieces in the Javorov sector during the opening days of the campaign. Ensuring that the southern flanks of 1.GD were covered, its sister division, 257.ID (Major General Sachs), resumed the attack from the Grodek–Kmienbrod–Dobrostany line (the sector described in the "Poland, 1939" chapter). On June 29, 1./GJR91 (Major Schneider) launched a *Kampfgruppe* in the direction of Lemberg (Lvov/Leopol/Lviv) along the main axis and ran up against strong resistance at Zimna Woda (Kaltwasser), the Soviet infantry being supported by heavy KV 2 tanks.

At the same time, also confronted by armor, GJR13, supported by artillery, and ensuring liaison with its neighboring division, the 257.ID, attacked to the south of GJR91. On June 30, the entire XXXXIX.Geb.-AK prepared for the attack on Lemberg, 4.GD in the end ensuring the opening to the south. The corps, indeed, gave priority to 1.GD, which had terminated the attack less than two years earlier, so it could enter the town first, on July 1. Except that this time round, there was no fighting as the Russians had abandoned the town, not before, however, massacring hundreds of civilians (*Volksdeutsche*, Ukrainians, Polish intellectuals) in the courtyard of the GPU prison. The Ukrainians welcomed the Germans as liberators and in turn instituted anti-Russian and anti-Jewish pogroms. (With reference to the "lightning raid on Lemberg", note the activities of one particular unit. Attached to I./Brandenburg, not mountain-specialized, was a battalion of Ukrainian volunteers, "*Nachtigall*" (nightingale), bringing together opponents of the Soviet regime. Nachtigall seems to have played an active part in the pogroms of Lemberg, initially assigned to the Polizei and the SS, and then organized into groups to keep order, acting with extreme cruelty, and destroying the image of liberators the German soldiers had fought so hard to attain.)

This combat sequence illustrates the principle, down to the lowest tactical echelon, of the "lightning war." During July, a *Vorausabteilung* from 1.GD (whose tactical insignia—the white edelweiss—is visible) with a PaK 37-equipped antitank section in the lead, has been taken to task by Soviet antitank guns (nicknamed "*Ratsch-Bumm*" by the Germans, lit. "ratchet cannon"). The gun teams position themselves and return fire, the following Sturmgeschütze then outflank the enemy, reduce the resistance, and enable the advance to resume. Note that the gun tractors are captured British MWD Bedfords. (Franz Moll Archives)

General Lanz was constantly shuttling between his units. Here he is with Geb.-Pi. Btl.54, his engineers' battalion. The *Oberfeldwebel*, Sergeant Major Baader, is on the left of the general and Captain von Raven, the *Oberkommando* of the Stab 1.GD is far right; both wear the M20 jacket inherited from the Reichswehr. (Franz Moll Archives)

By the close of June 1941, XXXXIX.Geb.-AK was force-marching on Lemberg. (Franz Moll Archives)

1.GD then went into the corps reserve and was able to rest for three days at Lemberg, whilst also providing antitank cover (Geb.-PJA44, Lieutenant Colonel Lang) at Winniki, where it drove off several Soviet attacks. 4.GD and 97.le.ID (Major General Maximilian Fretter-Pico) went into the lead in pursuit of the enemy. On July 3, 4.GD, 31 miles in front of 1.GD, took the village of Brzeczany. Sweeping aside any resistance, the division reached the Sereth (Siret) River, beyond which, on the 5th, it formed a bridgehead. On the 7th, it crossed the Zbrucz (Zbroutch) which marked the former Soviet–Polish border. Beyond that stretched the Ukrainian plains with an unknown—because it had only recently been established—obstacle: the Stalin Line.

1.GD dead were buried in common graves dug by the local populace. (Franz Moll Archives)

Gebirgsjäger and Lawall's *Radfahrer* search enemy vehicles along the route of the Soviet retreat, July 1941. (Franz Moll Archives)

During the night of July 3/4, 1.GD resumed its advance southeastward, via Winniki, the motorized Gruppe Lang in the lead while Major Lawall's *Radfahr-Abteilung* (cycle battalion) captured an armored train at Kopyczyne. During the evening of the 4th, Lang arrived in sight of the Soviet border, at Trembowla. The following day, he pressed on toward the Zbroutch River and the heights that dominated it on the opposite bank. The two *Jäger* regiments had trouble keeping up on foot. On the 12th, Vorausabteilung Lang and the 4.GD vanguard were in sight of the Stalin Line, the Soviet second line of defense—the first being, of course, the demarcation line in Poland—250 kilometers west of Lemberg.

In the morning of July 13, Kübler had his divisional commanders meet at 4.GD HQ, at Michalpol, to issue orders for breaking through the Stalin Line. Three divisions were to attack along a 37-mile front, the corps' sector: 97.le.ID to the north, 4.GD in the center, and 1.GD in the south. Kübler ordered a frontal assault against two-thirds of the line,

"Tag der Artillerie" (Day of the Artillery): the success of the attack against the Stalin Line was first and foremost the result of the artillery's effectiveness. Seen here are 15cm howitzers from IV/GAR79. (Franz Moll Archives)

The first obstacle in front of the Stalin Line was made up of minefields or mined strips which *Gebirgspioniere* tried to find with probes.

A wounded sapper is carried away by his comrades using tent canvas. (Franz Moll Archives)

The Stalin Line comprised a line of concrete strongpoints, separated by trenches and obstacles, two to three miles in depth. This bunker has been captured; a battalion *Stab* has just established itself with a portable radio set, a *Tornister-Funkgerät*.

the northern section being considered too difficult to penetrate. The 97th carried out a diversionary attack in the Rewuscha sector, thus drawing the enemy's attention and above all its artillery fire, and making the mountain units' task much easier. On the 13th and 14th, reconnaissance was undertaken, and the attack went ahead on the planned date, July 15, on both sides of the railway line, with two clear approaches.

Eglseer favored a frontal attack with his two *GJR*; with relatively light losses, the objective of the day—the Wolkowinzy–Warnyka road—was achieved. Lanz refused a frontal attack which, in view of the land and aerial reconnaissance, he considered potentially too costly. He ordered III./GJR99 (Major Hörtl) at the head of 1.GD to infiltrate an identified breach in the fortified positions, with the rest of his *GJR* following, along the corridor to deploy behind the fortifications and take the enemy from the rear. Hörtl was supported by the divisional artillery and the 8.8cm FlaK guns shooting through the embrasures. In 1.GD, July 15 thus became "*Tag der Artillerie*" (Day of the Artillery).

In the evening, the division also reached its objectives of the day. Lanz's refusal to resort to a frontal attack, going against the corps' orders, caused some coolness in his relations with Kübler, in spite of the operation's brilliant success. Results were indeed impressive: 40 strongpoints, eight artillery pieces, 10 machine guns, a tank, and three aircraft destroyed, with around 1,000 enemy killed and 286 taken prisoner. The Stalin Line, however, did not have the degree of sophistication of the Maginot or Metaxas Lines and collapsed more rapidly.

This lightning breakthrough—along 13½ miles of front in XXXXIX.Geb.-AK's sector—was considered by the Soviet command as the end of the battle of the borders. The Stavka removed everything in the path of the invaders, effecting a "scorched earth" policy, and leaving behind only delaying elements west of the Bug.

In 1.GD, it was III./GJR99 that "opened the door" for the rest of the division. Its commander, Major Hörl, is seen here immediately after the fighting. A mobile divisional HQ— in *Bergmütze*—are already preparing the next stage of the advance. (Franz Moll Archives)

The *Geb.-AK* therefore set off again, motorized *Vorausabteilungen* in the lead, the divisions following on foot and therefore at the speed of light infantry, sweeping aside enemy defenses, infantry or armor, taking advantage of the uneven terrain and forests, and utilizing supporting artillery fire.

The next objective, Vinnytsia (Winniza) on the Bug, at the southern limit of the Podoli Hills (of which the town was the capital), was achieved with 50,000 Soviet soldiers being captured. The region was very humid, the roads wretched and soaking. Attacking along the southern flank of the corps, 1.GD vanguards—Gruppen Lang and Wölflinger—arrived at the outskirts of the town; patrols reinforced by Sturmgeschütze reached the larger bridges in the town but found them blown.

4.GD remained blocked to the northwest, in contact with enemy units that had been tasked with delaying it. A further division was expected in theater, the 24.ID, to attack in the direction of Vinnytsia from the north and close the encirclement of the town. 1.GD remained where it was until July 21, watching the Soviets falling back east of the river without being able to intervene other than shelling the bridges and the improvised crossing sites farther north. The 15cm howitzers had no ordnance to fire to the required distance. The bulk of the enemy therefore escaped XXXXIX.Geb.-AK's clutches, this disappointment doing nothing to help relations between Kübler and Lanz.

With its *Radfahr-Abt.* (Lawall) and GJR99 (Kress), after hand-to-hand fighting, 1.GD succeeded in establishing a bridgehead on the Bug, at Brazlav (Braslav), to the south of Vinnytsia. It resumed its advance two days later after the neighboring units had realigned with it. XXXXIX.Geb.-AK., after this "failure"—after all, the operational objective had been to destroy or capture of the rest of the Soviet 6th and 12th Armies before they crossed the Bug—resumed its advance toward Uman. The 17th Army was obliged to pursue an elusive adversary across the vast Ukrainian expanses.

The hamlet of Galusincy, immediately behind the Stalin Line, was cleared after the assault and prisoners assembled. (DR)

After the battle of Uman, XXXXIX.Geb.-AK. rested. The *Reiter* of Geb.-Aufkl.-Abt.54 were forced to abandon their horses and dig themselves in in slit trenches. Note their riding boots (*Reitstiefel*). (Franz Moll Archives)

Oberjäger Moll, General Lanz's driver, responsible for many of the photographs in this book, takes a break on his Horch. (Franz Moll Archives)

4.GD, reinforced by the Slovak motorized brigade and followed by 97.Ie.ID, directed its axis of advance east-southeast and fought bitterly to capture Gaissin, Rossocha, Poporeloïe, and Maxinovka. With a constant threat on its unprotected southern flank of the corps—any enemy forces detected regrouping were dealt with by artillery and Stukas—1.GD seized a bridgehead over the River Sinica at Antonovka. When it was 20 or so miles south of Uman, on July 30, the OKH ordered it to abort its mission and link up with Kleist's Panzergruppe 1, engaged to the east of Uman, and where it was given the task of pivoting south around Babanka and Pervomaïsk. The division then advanced at speed to the southeast and Golovanesk which, in spite of stubborn heavy resistance, it took on July 31.

Gefreiter Kempter, a 1.GD photographer, fetches water from a well, accompanied by some local color. (Franz Moll Archives)

This I./GJR98 heavy machine-gun section has captured a Soviet 152mm howitzer. The victory has been claimed on the barrel with chalk. The helmeted *Obergefreiter* is carrying a haversack hooked onto his belt (or support) suspenders. (Franz Moll Archives)

1.GD preparing the next stage of operations, in the summer of 1941, on the Nogaic Steppe. General Lanz confers with his unit commanders. Lieutenant Colonel Lang, commander of Geb.Pz-Jg-Abt.44 is in the center. He has just been awarded the Knight's Cross. Also visible is Major Lawall, seen three-quarters rear, right. (Franz Moll Archives)

The first "*Hiwis*" (*Hilfswilligen*, auxiliary troops) were recruited in August 1941 on the Nogaic Steppe from among the Soviet prisoners, or, for certain non-combat duties like transport, from among the civilians. More and more of them started wearing an "*in the service of the Wehrmacht*" armband. (Private collection)

Kübler recognized how precarious the division's situation was, engaged alone, drawn out, and constantly being attacked along its flanks, in particular its baggage trains, by units of the Soviet 18th Army and 2nd Cavalry Corps; he therefore deployed his last reserves, 4.GD, on August 1 to "his" detached division: Colonel Pribyl's *Vorausabteilung* and Colonel Zimmer's *Pioniere* (Pionierestab 620—an organic unit of the corps). The same evening, Vorausabteilung Lang reached Troïanka and the great north–south axis along which the Soviet forces were trying to escape before encirclement in the Uman pocket.

On the 2nd, Lang attacked to the north in the Jatrani region, to join up with the armored force to the south of Temovka, thus closing the net. On August 3, the bulk of the division came up and the five divisions attacked Podwyssokoïe. Along a two-and-a-half-mile front, with its two *GJR* in the van, 1.GD launched its attack north; on its left, 4.GD had not been able to take Kopienkovata because it was strongly defended by units too firmly dug in. So it focused on Podwyssokoë from the southwest, with 97.le.ID fixing the Soviet forces on its left.

Pushing to the north of the *Kessel* (cauldron, or pocket) from west to east, 125.ID, 24.ID, and 297.ID drove off the remnants of the Soviet 6th and 12th Armies toward Podwyssokoïe, the net being closed by 16.ID(mot.) and 1. SS-Panzerdivision Leibstandarte SS Adolf Hitler.

Late during the night of August 5/6, about 4,000 Red Army troops, preceded by 10 or so armored vehicles tried to break out toward the south at the junction of 1. and 4.GDen, overwhelming 4.GD's rear HQ and causing casualties before being scattered and annihilated. The chief of staff of the Soviet 6th Army was captured.

By midday on August 7 , the battle of Uman–Podwyssokoïe was over, the Soviets leaving behind 22,000 troops, including three generals, more than 100 artillery pieces, and

By the beginning of fall, the *Gebirgsjäger* in this 8cm mortar team were wearing the heavy-cloth *feldgrau Mantel* (greatcoat). (Franz Moll Archives)

The fall rains made the roads progressively worse. The *leichter Heeresfeldkarren* (*Hf.1*), the light army field cart, in the foreground bears I./GAR79 and 1.GD (white edelweiss) markings. (Franz Moll Archives)

50 tanks. XXXXIX.Geb.-AK had a few days' rest and resumed its advance eastward on the 13th, easily outflanking Kirovograd by the south.

The countryside comprised rolling fields of cereals, vegetables, and cotton. People were generally reserved; some of them, descendants of the "Germans of the Volga" even spoke the invaders' language, sometimes seeing them as liberators. On August 20, the corps was already some 215 miles from the Uman battlefield but faced unexpected resistance around Vladimirovka, the Russians being given the task of slowing down the German forces so that a general withdrawal could be made to the east of Ingulez.

The next task, crossing the Dnieper, several kilometers wide in parts, was given to XXX.AK under von Manstein. XXXXIX.Geb.-AK went into the second echelon in order to prepare to exploit into the Nogaic Steppe. On September 1 and 2, XXX.AK succeeded in establishing a bridgehead on the Dnieper.

At the end of the battle of Uman, Kübler said, "without the 97.le.Div, breaking through [the Stalin Line, the advance] would not have been so rapid and the battle of Podvyssokoïe would not have been possible."

In the evening of September 2—*Pionier-Tag* (Day of the Pioneers)—engineers from XXXXIX.Geb.-AK, reinforced by Geb.Pi-Btl.54 of 1.GD and Pi.Btl-46, under the command of Pionier-Stab 620 (Colonel Zimmer), set up a 750-yard engineering construction composed of a 300-yard bridge and 450 yards of roadway sections ferried from an "assembly workshop" four-and-a-half miles upstream, all the while under attack from Soviet artillery and aircraft. The infantry crossings transpired over the next few days, without any protection from enemy fire.

At the head of the corps, 1.GD reached the opposite bank and made a dash eastward to widen the bridgehead held by 170.ID. The first village, Konstantinovka, was outflanked and then taken. Vorausabteilung Lang resumed the attack eastward, but ran into a counterattack at Marianov, its neighboring division (170.ID) being blocked at Antonovka. 1.GD was ordered to envelop this resistance from the south and destroy it. 4.GD, coming up behind 1.GD, then relieved Vorausabteilung Lang. The division with all its elements now brought together, resumed its eastward advance, took Rubanovka, and maintained contact with the Soviet rearguards. A GJR98 company, the 7th (von Hirschfeld), found itself encircled by a Russian unit during a reconnaissance and had to be rescued by the rest of II./GJR98 (Major Salminger). At Sofievka a GAR79 battery was attacked at night and badly mauled by an infantry battalion. The outflanking maneuvers proved they had their limits.

After crossing behind 1.GD, 4.GD hurried northeastward, pursuing the enemy in order to expand the army's maneuvering ability east of the Dnieper.

On September 19, XXXXIX.Geb.-AK's lead divisions, 1.GD, covering the northern flank of the corps, and 4.GD and 170.ID farther south, after an accelerated approach march, found themselves facing a major obstacle identified by the Luftwaffe as an immense antitank ditch in front of Timochevka, impossible to go round or take from behind. The only thing possible was a frontal attack, over very open terrain swept by heavy artillery fire.

On the 20th, after the usual artillery preparation, 1.GD *Jäger* with GJR98 on the left, went over to the attack. 8./GJR99 succeeded in infiltrating after hand-to-hand fighting, soon followed by the whole of II./GJR99. Soviet airpower and artillery fire in front of the German units was debilitating, especially the artillery, which, fortunately for the Germans, was beginning to run out of ammunition and fuel. GJR98, initially pinned down, ended up by getting III./GJR98 to advance, breaking through the half-mile-deep defensive disposition and reaching the edges of Timochevka, where it consolidated itself hedgehog-style.

The battalion was followed by the rest of the division under cover of darkness, which immediately established a defense on the other side of the ditch. Gruppe Lang captured a village farther north, Malaïa Belosïorka, in order to secure the northern flank. The Russians counterattacked all night but were unable to dislodge the Germans. 4.GD, which also had to drive off the Soviet attacks, launched a diversionary attack with GJR13 in the direction of Balki, while GJR91 (Colonel Ritter von Stettner) prepared to break out to the east of Malaïa Belosïorka.

Because of the two *GDen*'s heavy losses, the corps did not press the attack, all the more so as a new order arrived: after being relieved by the Romanian Mountain Corps, and initially making up a reserve for itself, XXXXIX.Geb.-AK had to quit the sector for another mission in the Crimea. The Soviets noticed these movements and became more aggressive, preventing the two *GDen* from breaking off.

In the trenches, the *Gebirgsjäger* remain vigilant, faced with Soviet attacks made easier by the frozen terrain. (Franz Moll Archives)

This reenactment using period equipment shows the two-piece camouflage suit adopted during the winter of 1941/2. Black identification stripes have been sewn on the sleeves to avoid friendly fire, since the Soviets wore the same sort of camouflage dress. The hip pockets of the jacket provide access to the uniform and equipment underneath, as does the loose buttoning down the front with only three buttons. The waist and the ankles of the overalls are fastened with wide canvas laces. The ski boots have hard, smooth leather soles, with reinforcement steel on the seams and a gully around the heel in order to hold the cable of the ski binding. (Private collection)

The Soviet elements that had been driven off by Panzergruppe 1 (von Kleist) after the battle of Kiev on the eastern banks of the Dnieper—on September 2—were advancing rapidly toward Balki, in fact transforming the withdrawal into an offensive in a sector made more fragile by the relief in progress.

In the morning of September 27, a day late after a forced march of 30 miles, 1.GD had barely arrived in the sector at Ivanovka—from which they would have to push on toward the Crimea—before halting its advance. On the 29th, conforming to XXXXIX.Geb.-AK's orders, it was rushed north, intending to drive back a strong enemy force. Losses were heavy, especially when facing the Stalin's organs, something new to the division. 4.GD didn't have time to break off completely as it was still untangling itself from the relief operation under way. It also had to take in Romanian elements suddenly retreating . 4.GD then disengaged so it could counterattack with a view to reestablishing the Malia Belosïorka–Balki Line.

On October 3, the Germans noticed weaker resistance and the following day, Soviet forces (18th Army) started falling back from the Timochevka antitank ditch after they failed to save the Crimea from the German invasion. Under the command of the 1st Panzer Army, XXXXIX.Geb.-AK started its pursuit eastward, in the direction of the industrial town of Stalino-Makeïeva (today Donetsk). In the Mogila-Tokmak region, between the Dnieper and the Sea of Azov, from October 8–10, it took part in completing the encirclement and destruction of the Soviet 18th Army: 100,000 troops fell into German hands.

The battlefield was an indescribable landscape of desolation, with innumerable vehicles and equipment scattered about. Soviet units in close order wandered aimlessly around, their officers on horseback seemingly lost and beaten.

Meanwhile fall had arrived, making any movement difficult. Apart from destroying the Soviet armed forces, the strategic objective had become the industrial installations and the enormous reserves of coal of the Donetz Basin, to be captured before the winter. 1.GD reached the region of Stalino (Donetsk) between October 11–17, without any major confrontation.

As the name of the town suggested (Stalin) the *Jäger* expected it would be difficult to take. They entered cautiously, and found the populace hostile—it comprised an authentic proletariat, fierce defenders of the communist system despite their wretched living conditions; many were those who slipped off to join the partisans—and the industrial installations wrecked. The division was positioned alongside the Italian "*Celere*" Division.

At the end of October, 1. and 4.GDen linked up and continued their advance—via Stepanovka, Amrossijevka, Removka, and Dimitrijevka—toward the Mius, about 45 miles to the north of Taganrog, a town situated at the mouth of a river on the Sea of Azov. The corps succeeded in crossing the river eastward where fighting was costly on both sides, against a determined adversary trying to gain time.

On November 5, I./ and III./GJR99, together with II./ and III./GJR98, crossed the Ovrag, a river that was already frozen and, not without difficulty, took the villages of Diakovo, Bobrikovo, and Platonovskoïe. The freezing temperatures transformed the fall sludge into concrete, immobilizing the armor and supply columns. The Soviets then tried to break through with several divisions between XIV. Panzerkorps and 1.GD so they could isolate III. Panzerkorps at Rostov which it had just taken. Faced with this situation, the 17th Army (Colonel General Hoth) ordered XXXXIX.Geb.-AK to fall back on the Mius and establish a defense for the end of November; this was done by December 2 with both *GDen*, and with 4.GD to the north. To its south, 1.GD had a Slovak brigade—which turned out to be particularly reliable—subordinated to it, together with the Wiking Division.

For its part, in early December, 97.le.Div was spread out over several sectors, under 17th Army's orders. Its two *Jäger* regiments were thus split up and the *Stab*, with the rest, set up at the junction of the 17th and 16th Armies. It only recovered its proper disposition in early April 1942 at the end of the *Winterschlacht* (winter battle).

As soon as it started snowing, priority was given to soldiers, vehicles, and animals to maintain freedom of movement. Dr Sebald, shown here, is getting his horses to advance along a logistics route (*Rollbahn*). (Franz Moll Archives)

At the end of February 1942, 1.GD transported elements by land, and by air too, in Junkers 52s, toward the Mius, where the Soviets had launched an offensive and broken through the Romanian positions. (Franz Moll Archives)

Kradmelderzug (the motorbike dispatch riders' section) of Stab 1.GD establishes its lines in Samara, and prepares to move its HQ, end April/early May 1942. (Franz Moll Archives)

In the spring of 1942, General Lanz assembled his officers, no doubt at the III./GJR98 HQ, whose command pennant is visible on the left. Von Hirschfeld, 2nd right, is recognizable, wearing a motorcyclist's oilskin. (Franz Moll Archives)

During the battle of the Bereka, large numbers of Soviet soldiers were killed, in the midst of their destroyed matériel. This Valentine tank, bogged down in the Bereka valley, was delivered by the British under the Lend-Lease Agreement to the Soviets. Another heavy vehicle, in the background, has suffered the same fate. (Franz Moll Archives)

Army Group Center's failure before Moscow had forced the Wehrmacht onto the defensive along most of the Eastern Front. Faced with the risk of the center collapsing, a limited reorganization of command was implemented and, on January 3, 1942. General Kübler took command of the 4th Army west of Moscow. Command of XXXXIX.Geb.-AK. was given to Lieutenant General Rudolf Konrad.

The opening of 1942 was marked by the worst crisis since the beginning of the campaign in the East, even since the beginning of the war. From December 19, 1941 onward, the Führer exhorted his troops to "fanatical resistance" (*fanatischer Widerstand*), with no thoughts of retreat. Sacking was the punishment for not respecting this general directive.

During early 1942 the Soviets made limited attempts to advance west of the Mius. The German divisions took advantage of this to get their personnel into better shape—

Field Marshal Fedor von Bock (facing the camera) visits 1.GD at the Bereka on May 28, 1942. Behind him some 10,000 Soviet prisoners are visible in the background. (Franz Moll Archives)

Portrait of a *Feldwebel*, a sergeant, and member of the *Kradmelderzug*. (Franz Moll Archives)

in particular affording them leave—and bring up to strength and repair all their matériel. A "historic" winter is only considered as really harsh when it is experienced by a large number of men living outside. This was the case for the entire Wehrmacht, which experienced temperatures dropping sometimes to -40°C. Basic equipment was inadequate and caused heavy losses, either dead or severely frostbitten.

The Soviets, with the experience gained in the Great North and in Siberia, were far better equipped and could endure operations of varying magnitude. Despite the extreme weather conditions, German units mostly held the positions they had taken, until the spring of 1942. They were rewarded with the *Winterschlacht im Osten* commemorative medal (Winter Battle in the East, nicknamed the "*Gefrierfleisch-Orden*"—the frozen meat medal).

On January 28, 1942, Army Group von Kleist was constituted, regrouping temporarily the 17th Army and the 4th Panzer Army in order to counterattack a massive Red Army winter offensive beyond the Donets, launched on January 18. The 17th Army's main depot was captured as the Soviets succeeded in breaking through some 75 miles. It was only in mid-February that this offensive was checked, but without the Germans retaking the terrain before the thaw, the *Rasputitsa*. On March 7, the Russians launched a new offensive east of Kharkov against positions held by the 6th Army; it was only stopped at the end of March, but which heralded the creation of Isium Salient west of the Donets.

It was in this context as a preventive measure that 1.GD left the Mius and XXXXIX. Geb.-AK, to be incorporated into III. Panzerkorps (von Mackensen) to stop the Soviet counteroffensive along the Samara, to the north of the Dniepropetrovsk–Stalino. It got there just before the Soviet vanguard—intending to recapture the Donbass (Operation *Barvenko-Lozovaya*)—and was able to establish favorable positions on relatively flat and, of course, completely frozen-over terrain. Until the end of March, intense fighting raged, 1.GD being reinforced by a battalion of tanks (the recently created Panzer-Abt.60), and an Italian brigade.

The arrival of the spring thaw transformed the roads and defensive positions into quagmires, hindering mobility and preventing either side from maneuvering, but in early May, violent winds dried out the ground, making movement practicable once again.

XXXXIX.Geb.-AK took part in the second battle of Kharkov, led by the 6th Army under General Paulus, from May 12–28. At dawn on the 12th, the Soviets launched an offensive on both sides of the Isium Salient, from Volchansk in the north and Barvenkovo to the south, thus outstripping the German operation. Initially on the defensive, the Germans regained the initiative due to strong support from the Luftwaffe—units taken temporarily from those supporting the 11th Army in the Crimea and the Kertch Peninsula—because this threat to *Fall Blau* had to be stopped. From the Alexandrovka sector, on May 17, III. Panzerkorps (von Kleist) and XXXXIX.Geb.-AK attacked the Barvenkovo bridgehead. 1.GD took part: at 0350, Angriffsgruppe Buchner (attack group Buchner, a reinforced GJR99) overwhelmed Soviet troops to the north of Alexandrovka, even though they were solidly dug in, without any major difficulty.

On May 19, Paulus attacked the Isium Salient from the north. On the 20th, 1.GD captured Gavrilovka, in the Isium sector, then attacked in the direction of Blisenzy against determined enemy resistance. From there, on the 24th, Whit Sunday, the division redeployed back north, transported in trucks. The Soviet forces, trying to fall back eastward to return to their main lines of defense, in the end found themselves encircled in several *Kessels*, including the valley of the Bereka, in the Losovenka region.

Fighting described by General Lanz as "causing shivers down my spine" took place until May 29: trying their luck in several directions, the Soviets attacked German positions in successive waves both during the day and at night; the attackers passed over the bodies of their comrades from the preceding waves, quite mad with drink, savagely fighting hand to hand with any available weapons—as in Great War—while Soviet vehicle pools and troops were strafed by the Luftwaffe. In all, the Soviets suffered between 240,000 and 277,000 casualties with mountains of equipment lost. German losses were 20,000. This bloodbath revealed the panic and incompetence of certain Russian command echelons. But the masses were already making up for the weaknesses of command which did later show great qualities at operational and strategic levels.

The Mountain Corps settled into defensive positions on the Donets and rested after burying its dead. On June 22, under XI.AK (Lieutenant General Strecker), itself subordinated to the 17th Army, 1.GD seized a bridge over the Donets, between Saliman and Savinzy, before it was completely destroyed—several *Jäger* from II./GJR98 were killed when it blew.

A *Jäger* in position facing the Donets, in a trench linking individual foxholes. He is armed with stick grenades and a Gewehr 33/40 with ZF41 (Zielfernrohr 41) sights. (DR)

To disengage from the Demyansk Pocket, Kampfgruppe Hoffmeister (7.GD) within 8.JgG, reinforced by tanks, attacked on skis to the south of Staraïa Russa in late March 1942. (DR)

Von Hirschfeld and II./GJR98 broke out of the bridgehead, captured Tchislovodovka then headed off toward Isium which the Radfahr-Abt. Lawall took in coordination with 97.le.ID which had been blocking all the town's exits to the south since the 17th. Fighting continued around Isium before the main force crossed the Donets. On the 27th, 1.GD reached a XXXXIX.Geb.-AK recovery zone around Barvenkovo.

At the beginning of May, admitting that *Barbarossa* was partly a failure, Hitler was certain, nonetheless, that the Red Army was at the end of its tether of its human resources and that seizing its logistic capabilities would administer the final fatal blow. He therefore ordered Army Group South's attack to be redirected toward the southeast (Stalingrad) and the south-southeast (the Caucasus), Operation *Siegfried* having evolved to *Blau* (blue) and then *Braunschweig* (Brunswick) on June 30. The strategic objective was to seize the oilfields and the industrial regions of Baku, at the southeastern tip of the Caucasus, Azerbaijan, which would in turn precipitate the collapse of the USSR.

Operations to take the fortress at Sebastopol began on June 7 and finished on July 7, with the Crimean Peninsula completely overrun. But Wehrmacht resources were now dangerously low.

Army Group North

In Army Group North, during *Barbarossa*, the only "mountain" elements engaged in 1941 were the Brandenburgers as mentioned earlier. The companies had been rapidly reorganized after the Balkan campaign and were in the van of the Wehrmacht offensive during the campaign against the Soviet Union. The 2nd Battalion was directed to Army Group North under Field Marshal von Leeb with its 7. and 8.(Geb.) Kp. Each army corps in the first echelon received a company. These *Jäger* wore Soviet smocks and trousers, or simply an overcoat over their German uniform, and approached their objectives in captured vehicles. The main effort was for a breakthrough along the Polish–Lithuanian border, to capture key points, the bridges in particular (notably on the Duna). By August, the companies had regrouped into their original garrisons for later action. As weather conditions at the end of the fall worsened, offensive operations bogged down.

However, lessons had been learned since 1939, as the Lehr Regiment Brandenburg zbV 800 missions were clearly defined in June 1942: lightning operations such as attacks, and sharp defensive or delaying operations. The Brandenburgers were theoretically organized into basic units of about 300 men, called companies, organized into two half-companies with two commando sections, or *Einsätze* (literally "actions"), and a heavy section.

In the spring of 1942, the *Rasputitsa* transformed the Volkhov region once again into a mass of quagmires and bogs, where the trees had been hacked down by artillery fire, as shown in this aquarelle by Hans Liska. (Private collection)

Each company was detached to an army group which, depending on its needs, assigned it to an army corps or to a division. Two liaison officers (VO, *Verbindungens-Offiziere*) were detached to the larger units utilizing them. This restructuring period also evolved, with fewer commando operations, and more constituted units with conventional uniforms, equipment, and weapons. The "dirty tricks" specialists, the former Freikorps veterans who had proved their worth until Operation *Barbarossa*, were assigned to a separate unit in the 1st Battalion.

Combat in Army Group North's sector was among the hardest and most costly the *Gebirgstruppen* were to experience, on terrain that was a far cry from their mountains.

Failure to capture Leningrad created a complicated situation: to the north the metropolis was blocked by the Finns; to the south and southeast, the encirclement was completed by the Germans. Lake Ladoga, and the eastern Baltic—the Gulf of Finland—were frozen during the winter and enabled troop movements and the besieged city to be supplied via the "road of life." Lake Ladoga and the sea were linked by the Neva River. To the east, flowing into Lake Ladoga was the Volkhov, a river that left Lake Ilmen and the eponymous town.

In December 1941, 5.GD (Major General Ringel) left Crete (see "The Balkans, Greece, and Crete, 1941" chapter), and reached its R&R area between Salzburg and the Tyrol to make up its strength, allow personnel to go on leave, receive new equipment and undertake training adapted to the new theater of operations. The initial planning was presented to the division: taking into account the fact that capturing Leningrad (besieged since September 1941) and its forward wartime port, Kronstadt, at the

Deployments were generally done by rail. Taking advantage of a stop, a *Gebirgsjäger* officer stimulates the local economy. (Lenz Archives)

mouth of the Neva River on the Gulf of Finland, could only be done in winter—the only season when the area could be driven across—the high command envisaged landing north of the city. The stakes were high: regaining the initiative from the Soviet Union that the United States and Britain had started supplying by sea, to inflict a resounding defeat on a symbolic city, and break up the *Murmanbahn*, the logistics route between Murmansk and Leningrad.

In mid-February, the division was deployed 80 or so miles to the west of the city to perfect its training, under orders of the 8th Army (Colonel General Georg Lindemann). But very quickly, the Soviets launched their winter offensive between the Neva and the Volkhov, forcing the Germans to abandon their plan. In mid-March 5.GD found itself spread out along the Neva, its battalions promised to the higher echelon and becoming what it called the *Rollbahn-Feuerwehr* ("the communication lines firemen"). I./GJR100 found itself at Mga, within 21.ID positions. Backup strongpoints were established, with fortifications made of logs, and mined obstacles swept by machine guns on fixed firing lines. The large open spaces were covered by patrols on skis, with skirmishes, ambushes, and raids being the defensive weapons of choice.

The arrival of spring and the *Rasputitsa*, the thaw and its muddy corollary, did not allow for any movement in and around the bog which the division occupied, and which gave them their nickname, *Sumpfjäger* (marsh hunters), in a region infested by mosquitos.

It was only at the beginning of July 1942 that, in order to break the encirclement of Leningrad, the Soviets regained the initiative between Schlüsselburg, the shores of Lake Ladoga, and the Volkhov, then along this same river up to Lake Ilmen and Novgorod (second and third battles of Ladoga). Their attacks, however, bogged down and ended in *Kessels*, encircled and then destroyed one after the other at the end of the month.

At the beginning of 1942, leaving the camp at Grafenwöhr, the new 7.GD (formerly 99. Jäger-Division, commanded by the Austrian, Major General Martinek) also reached the southern sector of Leningrad, along the Neva and Lake Ladoga, in the forests and marshes of the Volkhov, and to the south of Lake Ilmen, with several of its units (the rest were sent to the Karelian front, in the Uthua sector).

Indeed, on March 16, 1942, Kampfgruppe Hoffmeister—GJR206, III./GJR218, and I./GAR82—arrived at a position some 40 kilometers from Lake Ilmen in the Staraï Russa region.

The commander of XXXXIX. Geb.-AK, Lieutenant General Konrad, visits 1.GD in the wooded Teberda Valley in the Caucasus. Major Lawall (right) commander of the *Vorausabteilung* made up around his divisional *Radfahr-Abt*, listens in. (Franz Moll Archives)

It was -35°C. The *Kampfgruppe* first joined 122.ID, subordinated to X.AK, then 8.JgD, and on March 21 took part under its command in *Unternehmen Brückenschlag* (Operation *Bridgelaying*), 40 or so kilometers south of Staraï Russa. The objective was to break the encirclement of II.AK, surrounded in the Demyansk Pocket, with an attack by Stossgruppe Seydlitz, a shock group made up of several divisions or equivalent.

With temperatures dropping already, movement was difficult and the artillery shells didn't always explode. On March 28, the *Kampfgruppe*, on skis, attacked a Soviet detachment set up in a clearing in a wood. Soon the battlegroup found itself in trouble, with heavy losses, facing an adversary both fleeting and well protected by fortified and well-camouflaged positions.

On April 3, subordinated this time to 5.JgD, Kampfgruppe Hoffmeister attacked in the direction of Ramuchevo. The thaw was starting; sludge slowed down all movement while being less practicable even for skiers, artillery pieces were immobilized, and mules drowned. Artillery support was problematic: on complex terrain with few maps, sight settings were made sometimes by sound (by ear!), while Stalin's organs spewed out murderous counter-battery fire. Supply routes were regularly cut by the Soviets who were set up in well-protected lines of defense around the Staraïa Russa–Ramuchevo road. The attack, launched on April 5 by the *Kampfgruppe*, progressed slowly in the melted snow and bogs, faced with determined Russian counterattacks supported by tanks, and concluded with a Phyrric victory on the 11th.

Kampfgruppe Hoffmeister then established a defense in the Redzy region, on the Lovat, where it fought in extreme conditions until the end of April. The *Jäger* used the shot-down trees to lay makeshift roads, tree trunks fastened together called *Knüpeldämme* ("bludgeon routes"). On April 29, it linked up with units from II.AK and the encirclement of the Demyansk Pocket was broken.

Until the end of May, without any real pause in the fighting, the *Jäger* reinforced their positions, reestablishing the continuity of their positions within II.AK. In early June, they attacked in the direction of the Gridino "track" and took the Soviet positions before setting up their defenses. Stossgruppe Seydlitz had accomplished its mission. On June 28, 1942, the battle of the Volkhov was over. Among the 33,000 Soviet prisoners was a senior Red Army officer, General Vlassov, commander of the 2nd Army.

Vorausabteilung Lang reaches Rostov-on-Don in August 1942 without firing a shot. Elements of 1.GD followed by train. (Lenz Archives)

Sonderverband Bergmann

Sonderverband (Special Group) Bergmann was the first unit of mountain troops in the German armed forces recruited abroad. The order constituting this "special (with a special vocation) unit" of the Wehrmacht and its command was issued by the OKW/Amt Ausland on October 14, 1941 to *Oberleutnant der Reserve* (Reserve Lieutenant) Professor Dr Theodor Oberländer, who had been an advisor in setting up the Nachtigall battalion, and who at the time, was the intelligence officer for the German Government General in the Ukraine. But it was the Abwehr II, the secret services department under Admiral Canaris in charge of sabotage and recruitment of foreign volunteers, that piloted its establishment so that a certain amount of secrecy was guaranteed, including from the Führer, who didn't at the time approve of recruiting Slav volunteers. This unit was to open the gates to the Caucasus and prepare a people's uprising against the Soviets in this mountainous region.

The first elements were assembled at Neuhammer Camp in Silesia, under the cover of the Bau-Lehr-Bataillon zbV 800 Brandenburg (and therefore of Admiral Canaris who visited the unit on July 7 and 8, 1942) using Georgian, North Caucasian, Armenian, and Azeri volunteers, selected mainly from among Soviet prisoners through an intensive "psychological" operation. Some of the officers, however, were Caucasians who had immigrated to France after the Russian Civil War. Caucasian nationalist and anti-Soviet sentiments were used to recruit soldiers.

On March 26, 1942, the Bergmann left Neuhammer for the training camp Hochgebirgsschule Luttensee, near Mittenwald, to perfect its mountain training. Oberländer's assistant, Sonderführer W. von Kutschenbach, who had grown up in Russia, spoke fluent Russian and Azeri. Administratively, this *Sonderverband* was incorporated in the Bergkaukasien Legion then the Nord-Kaukasien Legion, but in practice, it received its orders from the Abwehr or from Abwehr units incorporated in the Heer.

On July 25, 1942, considered as trained and trustworthy, Sonderverband Bergmann transferred to the Caucasus. The unit boasted a strength of 1,200: 300 Germans—themselves volunteers coming mainly from the Bergwacht, an association of volunteer mountain rescue teams attached to the Polizei—and 900 Caucasians, and organized into five ethno-linguistic companies: 1./, 4./ and 5./Georgians (5./ with an Armenian section); 2./ North Caucasians; and 3./ Azeris. In August 1942, during the fighting in the North Caucasus, new volunteers—among whom were recent deserters from the Red Army—enabled four companies of fusiliers to be formed. Three squadrons of Cherkessk cavalry joined on October 8, 1942: 7./ with 145 troopers, 8./ with 152, and 9./ with 162 troopers. At the end of October 1942, the three squadrons were subordinated to III. Panzerkorps. A 10./ Georgian company with 252 troopers, and an 11./ with 252 Azeri troopers, swore allegiance after being recruited in the North Caucasus, in the Cherkessk region. A depot, 13.Kp., with 400 troopers was also formed.

The *Sonderverband* gradually reached 2,690 men, of whom 240 were Germans spread throughout the battalions. As at August 22, 1943 the breakdown was: I./ (Captain Brand) with an HQ company and companies 1.–4.; II./ (Captain Mertelsmann) HQ and 5.–8.; III./ (Major Horstmann) HQ and 9.–12.; as well as two heavy companies (13. and 14.) of the Nordkaukasisches Infanterie-Btl. The transfer of I.(kauk) Luftwaffen-Feld-Bataillon and its 270 North Caucasian volunteers to the Sonderverband Bergmann on March 26, 1943, contributed to this increase in strength.

Machine-gunners wearing the *kindjal* on the *Bergmütze*, the symbol of Sonderverband Bergmann.

The first engagements took place in the Piatigorsk region in the latter part of 1942. The 2nd Company (Dagestan recruits) went through their baptism of fire on August 28 in the Malka valley, near Gundelen, while reconnoitering toward the unit's objective: to reach the Georgian military road (*grusinische Heerstrasse*) and from there to Tbilisi (Tiflis). This objective was never achieved, the German forces having halted on the Terek. Several Bergmann units were engaged in the fight against partisans in the Mozdok–Kalchik sector.

In September 1942, an airborne commando of 25 men, Germans and Chechens under the command of an *Oberleutnant*, First Lieutenant Lange, a Brandenburger, was formed within the Sonderverband Bergmann. Parachuted by order of the Abwehr behind the Soviet lines in the Grozny region to gather information and carry out acts of sabotage, they acted in unison with a Chechen uprising, seizing oil refineries around Grozny (Operation *Schamil*), while waiting for the bulk of the German armored forces which were supposed to break through between September 25 and 27. But they never made it, which meant the commando was forced to fall back toward friendly lines with heavy losses.

In October, the *Sonderverband* was engaged on operations in the Natchik and Terek (Ischerskoïe) regions, in the mountains and then on the steppes. The winter was particularly harsh but the battalion coped. From January 1, 1943, Bergmann started to fall back on the Crimea via the Kuban Plain and the Peninsula of Taman, covering the general withdrawal of the German armies threatened with encirclement following the defeat at Stalingrad. On February 22, it assembled at Bakhchisaray, in Crimea. The *Stab* settled in the summer hunting lodge of Prince Yussupov, at Kokkosi. Soviet agents, however, managed to infiltrate the *Sonderverband* and very nearly persuaded the volunteers to desert en masse. But the Geheime Feld Polizei (GFP) arrested three officers, three aspirants, two NCOs, and four soldiers, tried and judged them and had them executed.

From June 1943 to February 1944, the *Sonderverband* fought in Crimea as a reserve for Army Group A. The November 17, 1943 *Wehrmachtbericht* (army communiqué) evoked I./ and III./s' exemplary defense of Perekop. In the fall of 1943, II./ received some Azeris and its North Caucasians formed III./. In February 1944, the *Sonderverband* was split up for the first time: II./ (Azerbaijan) fought in LXXXII.AK of the 6th Army/Army Group A in the Ukraine, along the River Bug.

On March 12 it joined the divisional depot of foreign volunteers (Freiwilligen-Stamm-Division) at Mende in France. In August, it moved to Poland and took part in suppressing the Warsaw insurrection in the Dirlewanger Division/9th Army. It followed the 9th Army withdrawal until March 1945, suffering heavy losses in the process. Merging with the rest of I./111 (Aserbaidschanes) Bataillon of 111.ID—also coming from the Caucasus, Warsaw, and East Prussia—on March 27, 1945, the unit formed III./Grenadier-Regiment 1607 of the 599. (russische) Brigade of Vlassov's army, defending the coast west of Denmark.

For their part, in March 1944, I./ (Georgien) and III./(NordKaukasien) were withdrawn from XXXXIX.Geb.-AK of 17th Army/Army Group A and deployed to the south of Greece and subordinated to LXVIII.AK in Army Group E. They remained there until September 1944. I./ was then subordinated to 11. Feld-Division (Luftwaffe) in Athens and then in Macedonia. III./ reached Megara in Greece, joining 181.ID at the end of September. Both battalions were engaged in the region of Visegrad, southwest of Sarajevo. In March 1945, I./ joined XXXIV.AK in Smyrna, and III./ the LXXXX.AK in Slovenia. On February 12, 1945, the Stab Sonderverband Bergmann as well as 13./ and 14/. Schwadron were disbanded, the battalions continuing the fight independently. At the end of the war, I./ was captured by the Yugoslavs, and II./ and III./ by the British. All the volunteers as well as some German officers were handed over to the Soviets. Few survived.

The *Kindjal*

The Caucasian knife, the *kindjal*.

The symbol chosen for Sonderverband Bergmann was the *kindjal*, a short traditional Caucasian dagger. Made of light metal, with a first series of 1,100 examples (a second one with 2,500 examples was made in August 1943) numbered on the reverse side (the number was inscribed in the soldier's *Soldbuch*, or paybook), it was issued to all personnel. The German personnel also bore the mountain troops' edelweiss. Well-informed Soviets tried to carry out a commando operation, parachuting behind German lines to put the Stab Bergmann out of action and the commandos wearing German dress wore the insignia. Later, in Soviet captivity, veterans were urged to stop wearing the *kindjal*, and to tear out the page mentioning it had been issued to them, or even destroy the whole *Soldbuch*, to try and escape death.

The Bergmann nationality escutcheons

Even if, according to the veterans, wearing them was not systematic, the nationality escutcheons shown here were worn: *Nordkaukasien* (North Caucasus), *Aserbaidschan* (Azerbaijan), *Armenien* (Armenia), and *Georgien* (Georgia)

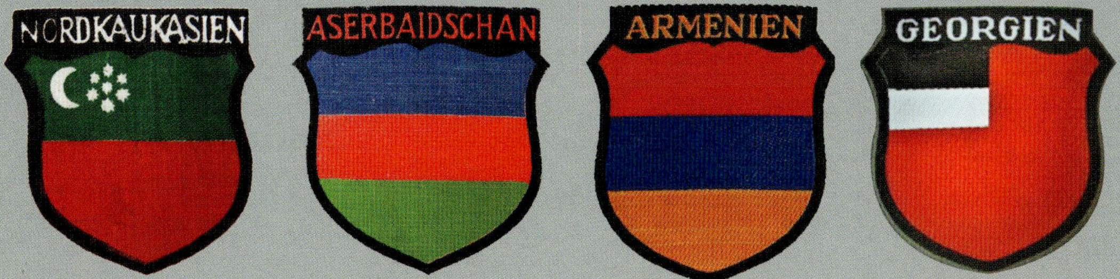

Norway and Finland, 1941–42

After the French and British Expeditionary Corps had left, the German high command defined an occupation zone as far as Kirkenes on the border with Finland. The two mountain divisions, 2.GD under Feuerstein and 3.GD under Dietl then Kreysing, were grouped together within the Gebirgskorps Norwegen under the command of General Dietl, who began a thorough reconnaissance of his area of operations in order to find any possible billets, HQs, and coastal battery emplacements.

The corps' first HQ was set up in a small cruise ship that ferried passengers between Norway and Sweden, the *Black Watch*, anchored in the Kaafjord. Within five weeks, the entire corps had been transported by land, air (including flying boats), and sea to the occupation zone which extended from Hellemobotn on the Arctic Circle to Kirkenes. With the chances of Germany attacking the USSR—*Unternehmen Rentier* (Operation *Reindeer*)—increasing, the Mountain Corps in particular took into account the risk of Finland being threatened again, as it had been during the Winter War at the end of 1939.

Under command of *General der Gebirgstruppe*, General Dietl, the Mountain Corps Norwegen (XIX.Geb.-AK) moved two mountain divisions, 2.GD (Major General Ernst Schlemmer) and 3.GD (Major General Kreysing) and its organic units between April and June 1941 by sea and land to the Varingerfjord region (*Unternehmen Blaufuchs I & II*, operations *Blue Fox*). From there, and with agreement from the Finnish government, German columns were present on the frontier between Norway and Finland on June 22, 1941—the date of the German offensive, Operation *Barbarossa*, along the length of the Eastern Front from the North Sea to the Black Sea (the far northern component being *Unternehmen Silberfuchs*—Operation *Silver Fox*, conducted by AOK (Armeeoberkommando) Norwegen under Colonel General von Falkenhorst).

Following on from the campaign in the spring of 1940 in Norway, the outstanding personality that emerged in the Great North of Europe was Lieutenant General Eduard Dietl, commanding XIX.Geb.-AK, or Armeekorps Norwegen. When Operation *Polarfuchs* (Arctic Fox) opened, the general commanding XXXVI.Geb.-AK was *General der Kavalerie*, General Hans Feige. (DR)

Gebirgstruppen occupied strongpoints all along the North Sea coast including the Arctic Circle. Captured Norwegian equipment—furs and weapons—was particularly appreciated.

On the heights, strongpoints were set up using the region's basic material, stone. (Ehrt Archives and DR)

Whether training or reconnoitering the terrain, patrols were, of course, carried out on skis. (DR)

Captain Günther was an officer in an unidentified staff or logistics unit. He is most likely the author of the photos credited to the Ehrt Archives. His hobby gives us a rare opportunity to look at a page in the history of the Northern Front. The clarity of his pictures enables us to appreciate a wide range of *Gebirgstruppe* activities. The rigid pennant on the vehicle indicates an officer's car. (Ehrt Archives)

The corps crossed the Petsamo region to move into Russia at daybreak on June 29 in the Titowka region. *Unternehmen Platinfuchs* (Operation *Platinum Fox*, part of *Silberfuchs*), the attack by Geb.-AK Norwegen toward Murmansk, opened on the shores of the White Sea, and was the most northerly operation of the Eastern Front.

Geb.-AK Norwegen was confronted with a peculiar situation: it had no neighbors—to the north the White Sea, to the south a 375-mile expanse of tundra and forest before the next unit of any significance, XXXVI.Geb.-AK, which was attacking toward Salla. The logistical supply routes between the Fatherland and the Kirkenes base were directly threatened by the Royal Navy over a distance of 200 nautical miles.

The corps' mission was to capture the town and port of Murmansk, at the end of the Bay of Kola (to the south of the eponymous peninsula, in the estuary of the Tuloma River) on the Barents Sea (Eismeer), ice-free throughout the year; then block the land route between Murmansk and the White Sea, then the *Murmanbahn*, the railroad between Murmansk and Leningrad, all to interdict Allied deliveries of matériel to the Soviets by sea.

This group of officers is taking advantage of the pleasant short summer season in occupied territory. Note the variety of the cuts and tints of the jackets. (Ehrt Archives)

Subsequent experience was to show how pertinent this choice was, as about a quarter of the Western Allies' support came through Arkhangelsk and Murmansk, the rest arriving via the Persian Gulf or Vladivostok.

As the distance to be covered was only 75 miles, the German command foresaw no major difficulty but it underestimated certain key factors. Dietl hoped to reach Murmansk in three days. However, a blitzkrieg was almost impossible: no communication axes, transport on muleback and advancing only on foot, difficulty moving artillery and armor, fighting partisan-style tactics, and facing a new enemy who turned out to be particularly motivated. The few maps available lacked any useful information anyway. So this "expeditionary corps" had to find a way of functioning without armor or vehicles. Logistics routes had to be set up in the rear; only the Luftwaffe provided a more modern aspect. Apart from the basic qualities of their troops, the Soviets could rely on a fairly dense network of overland communications as well as almost total control of the sea routes, and of the coasts, inlets, and bays of the Barents Sea and the White Sea. AOK Norwegen comprised two German and one Finnish army corps.

After the fighting, almost systematically, German commanders organized sporting events aimed at physical fitness and cohesion. Here we see two events, one with a start line, the other with a finish line (*Ziel*—lit. target), decked out with *Reichskriegflaggen*. (Ehrt Archives)

Double-breast-pocketed anoraks fitted with drawstrings were issued, available before the war in limited numbers to the mountain training schools. (Ehrt Archives)

Geb.-AK Norwegen, reinforced by Finnish border units, attacked along two axes, starting in the Petsamo region and appearing on the Russo-Finnish border: 3.GD to the south and 2.GD to the north, on either side of Kuosmejärvi, had to cross the Titowka, capture the fortified heights to the northeast of Tsorjärvi on the northern tip of the Stalin Line, then continue the breakthrough to the Motowski–Zapahnaïa Liza road. The terrain turned out to be more difficult than foreseen, rocky along the coast, and tundra (a mineral quasi-desert alternating with a myriad of lakes) with no landmarks. The first phase proved successful for the Germans: they crossed the River Titowka and pushed the enemy back onto the isthmus of the Rybatchi Peninsula, the *Fischerhalbinsel*.

But by early July, morale was being affected by supply difficulties as the Germans resigned themselves to establishing defensive positions along a 35-mile-wide front over very difficult terrain. All attempts to resume the advance failed. Dietl asked for reinforcements. He was assigned 6.GD (whose transport by sea was interrupted by the Royal Navy, with the result that they were only able to arrive in October), with SS-Infanterie-Regiment 9 and IR.388 (from ID.214 stationed in Norway) arriving from Norway. Despite insufficient initial reserves, Dietl resumed his operation on September 8, but it was another failure with heavy losses, notably for the Waffen-SS, who were insufficiently trained in Arctic conditions and poorly equipped. On September 22, blocked on the Liza, its "river of destiny", without being able to break out of the bridgehead and take the heights to the southeast of the river before the arrival of winter, Gebirgskorps Norwegen halted its advance and set itself up in defense, 35 or so miles from Murmansk, thus marking the end of Operation *Platinfuchs*.

The commander of 3.GD, Major General Hans Kreysing, wears a greatcoat with red lapels and gold buttons and sporting a voluminous fur collar. In the center is Major Schlebrügge (facing), commander of I/GJR139 and a pioneer in developing ski units.

This *Oberjäger*, or sergeant, having a break after the initial fighting on the Stalin Line, has been recently promoted: the spurs of the *Obergefreiter* stripes are still visible and NCO's collar *Tresse* have not as yet been sewn on. The sports insignia, his only decoration, shows he has not spent much time at the front. His MPi magazine holders are made of canvas. (Ehrt Archives)

Dietl had to report to OKW that he was at the end of his tether, simply taking into account his already very weak numbers. 2. and 3.GDen, later reinforced with other units, soon proved quite unsuitable for the mission because of their equipment and their paucity of supplies. XXXVI.Geb.-AK under *General der Kavallerie*, General Feige, however identified alternative terrain for Operation *Arctic Fox* with Kampfgruppe Nord in the center; 169.ID to the north and Finnish elements to the south were engaged between Rovaniemi and Salla, aiming at Kantalahti and Kandalashka, where the *Murmanbahn* came out at the White Sea, to the south of the Kola Peninsula, then at the *Murmanbahn* toward Murmansk. Salla was taken on July 8 but momentum stopped at a very humid, almost-inaccessible Kayrala.

The advance then resumed. The vanguard of Kampfgruppe Nord reached Alakurtti on September 1, then the former pre-1940 Russo-Finnish border. The heights above Lake Tolwand and those above the Werman Lakes (Upper and Lower), together with the Tuntsa Joki River, comprised the limit of the German advance and the corps established a defense. The geography alternated between tundra and primary forest, very humid and barely penetrable.

The Finnish III Corps under General Siilasvuo on the other hand, appearing in the Suomusalmi region 155 miles farther south, advanced more easily and began a series of outflanking maneuvers. On August 7 it reached Kestenga before continuing eastward. But the advance broke down in front of Uhtua, the Pjä, and Top Lakes. Kampfgruppe Nord came up in reserve. On October 30, the attack resumed east of Kestenga. Fighting lasted until November 13; on the 17th, the Finnish high command decided to call off the attack, midway between Kiestinski and the *Murmanbahn*, at Kilometer 32, the farthest extent of the Finno-German advance.

This *Gefreiter* (Pfc) takes advantage of a pause to fill up his flask (*Feldflasche*). (Franz Moll Archives)

Shortly before winter, which began in fact in October, 3.GD was relieved by 6.GD—itself relieved from its occupation mission in the Balkans, having arrived too late to play a role—but leaving behind GJR139 which later made up Gruppe Kräutler. Its arrival had no bearing on the offensive being resumed; its role was soon limited to holding captured positions, the bridgeheads across the Liza, alongside 2.GD which secured the positions toward the south that were empty of enemy troops.

The winter conditions prevented even the Finns and the Norwegians embarking on military operations, considering that large units could not hold out too long north of the Arctic Circle. However, General Ferdinand Schörner, commander of 6.GD, energetically attempted to find logistical solutions in order to continue supporting the frontline troops.

The OKW then called off the offensive in this sector, limiting the mission to holding the territorial gains critical to the German war economy, because of the exceptional nickel mines at Kolosjoki in the Petsamo Province (as well as copper and molybdenum resources). The war in the Great North had changed into a war of position, in the snow and the ice from October to May inclusive, with frozen lakes and marshes, weak light, and the sun shining only briefly. Murmansk was never taken. This front became a secondary front, and was of no interest until the fall of 1944 when it was a question of withdrawing all German troops from Finland after it switched sides.

Appointed *Oberbefehlshaber*, commander-in-chief, in Lapland (AOK Lappland) on February 2, 1942, Dietl organized the 20. Gebirgsarmee, the new name given to AOK Lappland on June 22, defining three sectors (*Abschnitte*): in the south Abschnitt Louhi, Gen.-Kdo.XVIII.Geb.-AK (General Böhme) who had relieved the Finnish III Corps at the beginning of 1942, with 7.GD and the 6.SS-Gebirgsdivision Nord, in the Toposero and Pjawosero region; the area was Karelian primary forest, with very few roads (the Germans therefore had to make them, in particular using *Knuppeldämme*) that alternated between thick woods with abrupt granite cliffs, and flooded and marshy zones, infested with mosquitos in the summer months. In the center, with similar terrain, was Abschnitt Kandalakcha: Gen.-Kdo. XXXVI.Geb-AK, with two infantry divisions, 163. and 169.ID. In the north was Abschnitt Murmansk: Gen.Kdo XIX.Geb.-AK with 2. and 6.GDen where the terrain was more complex—rocky, very uneven coast broken by fjords, cliffs, and tundra.

To enable the troops facing the Red Army to set off on June 22, 1941, units from AOK Norwegen were transported through Finland by road in military and requisitioned vehicles—spring and the disappearance of the snow allowed road transport to be used extensively—or on foot or skis, where necessary.

Petsamo became the German operational and logistics hub until 1944. The 2.GD reindeer's head is visible on the truck door. (Ehrt Archives)

Two officers check out their start line on the Russo-Finnish border, June 21, 1941. The *Hauptmann* (captain) on the left is wearing an edelweiss on the right sleeve of his *Windjacke*. (Ehrt Archives)

Just after midnight on June 29, 1941, a week after the launch of *Barbarossa*, elements of GJR138 crossed the icy waters of the Titowka River, in shorts, at the northernmost tip of AOK Norwegen's offensive line. (Ehrt Archives)

The extension northward of the Stalin Line is illustrated here: the heights to the east of the Titowka were fortified, with concrete, or stone and concrete bunkers. (Ehrt Archives)

An officer observing the terrain from the turret of a burned-out amphibious Soviet T-38 tank. This type of machine was useful in lake and fjord regions. The German vehicle on the extreme right is still whitewashed for winter. (Ehrt Archives)

Troops and mules advance over rocky ground following the seizure of the Stalin Line. (Ehrt Archives)

AOK20 settled at Rovaniemi, with Colonel General von Falkenhorst proceeding to Oslo. Dietl's role was liaison between the political (President Ryti, Prime Minister Rangell) and military (Marshal Mannerheim) authorities. But he remained in contact with his troops, often visiting far-flung outposts in all weather. Hitler visited the front on the occasion of the 75th birthday of the hero of Finnish independence, Marshal Mannerheim, and appointed Dietl major general.

Between the Kandalakcha and Murmansk sectors, terrain prevented the Soviets from making any kind of offensive maneuvers, and from the summer of 1942 onward, the Finnish Border Chasseurs were able to cover an area of land several hundred miles wide. Later, they were joined by five battalions of fortress infantry (210.ID), a Luftwaffe regiment, Gruppe Kräutler, and eight coastal artillery batteries placed under Seekommandant (Naval Command) Kirkenes.

By the first winter, the 20. Gebirgsarmee area of operations turned out to be the most difficult of the whole Eastern Front in terms of logistic support, in particular for XIX. Geb.-AK, the farthest north. Because there were no map indications, German troops gave names to the terrain redolent of their alpine origins: for summits and lakes, Hausberg, Edelweisskuppe, Steinkogel, and Winkelsee.

The "winter battle of 1942" was launched by the Soviets at the beginning of April with start dates varying according to the sectors, and depending on the thaw. The German positions held fast over the whole front. General Ferdinand Schörner, a harsh disciplinarian, had just taken command of XIX.Geb.-AK. Stavka's intention was to cut off 6.GD from the rear of the AOK and to take Petsamo on May 1 to mark International Day of the Proletariat. 6.GD, which had positioned its supporting strongpoints around the Liza River and Motowski Bay, was attacked that day by Red Army troops landing on the Rybatchi Peninsula to the west of the Liza. Elements of 2.GD in the corps' second echelon reacted west of the Titowka, with GJR139 in reserve with Abschnitt Louhi. The fighting lasted until the May 5, with the Soviet 12th Marine Infantry Brigade by then almost encircled. However, three days of Arctic snowstorms, late but violent, put paid to any fighting and allowed some Russian soldiers to reach their lines. This was the last intensive fighting in this sector until 1944.

In SS-Kampfgruppe Nord, a number of men from other units wore the forage cap (*Schiffchen*, here the first version with the metal death's head), like this *Sturmmann* (lance corporal) commenting on a Soviet news sheet. He has also attached a Finnish cockade to the side of his headdress. (DR)

General Dietl visiting the Karelia Front, late June 1941. Accompanied by a Finnish colonel—probably a member of the liaison detachment—he has, it seems, just reviewed the military situation at Colonel Hofmeister's GJR136 command post.

The *Oberleutnant* holding the map case is Dietl's aide-de-camp, First Lieutenant Krause. The officer accompanying the Finnish colonel is carrying the traditional *puukko* knife. (Ehrt Archives)

Lakes and fjords caused problems for the infantry and baggage trains. (Ehrt Archives)

As the fall set in, German units established their defensive lines. (Ehrt Archives)

Rebadged 7.GD on November 13, 1941, as its first mission, 99.le.ID was ordered to prepare for a winter engagement in Finland. This division had taken part in the fighting in the Ukraine, and troops already bore the green of the *Jäger*, the *Bergmütze*, while its divisional insignia represented the *Bergschuhe*, the mountain boots with fly's wings.

What remained was to adopt the edelweiss and train the men for the Arctic operational area, undertaken in Bavaria by Finnish instructors. The ski training was particularly specialized; the necessary equipment, like items of warm clothing, came from donations from the local populace. Training with mules and sledges, and artillery firing took precedence. In January 1942, the detachment left camp at Grafenwöhr for Stettin, the Baltic, and Finland.

This IR388 sniper covers the arrival of 6.GD, with his Mauser with ZF39 telescopic sights. (Ehrt Archives)

Despite use of Finnish icebreakers, the sea was frozen, a portent of the winter harshness and the consequent transport difficulties. There were significant matériel losses: the GJR218 antitank company went to the bottom with the merchant ship *Helgoland*. Only two GJR218 battalions, Rgt-Stab and Geb.-Pi.-Kp.99, reached Finland, at Hango, 100 kilometers west of Helsinki, where they were committed to the Uthua sector alongside the Finnish 11th Infantry Regiment. They went into action almost immediately.

The rest of the division, under a temporary commander, only left Grafenwöhr at the beginning of March, for an unknown destination. Kampfgruppe Hoffmeister—made up mainly of GJR206, III./GJR218, and I./GAR82—was incorporated into 122.ID and took part in the relief of the Demyansk Pocket. With the end of this successful mission, the *Kampfgruppe* left on July 16 for Finland where it joined III. and IV./GAR82 engaged on the Volkhov.

Departing Grafenwöhr in early May, and disembarking at Hango, other 7.GD units reached the logistics base at Hyrinsalmi established during the winter, by train before continuing on foot on tracks made along the Lietinski Front. Kampfgruppe Hoffmeister was still in the Lake Ilmen sector, with two GJR218 battalions under 122.ID. Gruppe Krakau (Major General Krakau) was deployed to relieve Kampfgruppe Nord, overwhelmed by a Soviet attack to its north and comprised GJR139, IR307, Geb.A.A.99, Geb.Pi.Btl.99, and a group of mixed artillery—Geb.Art. and light recoilless howitzers—under orders of GAR82 (Colonel Freiherr van der Hoop). Alongside a Finnish unit, they drove off the Soviets between May 16–25 before taking the *Gebirgsjäger* route (an artificial gap in the forest between Kiestinski and Lake Jeletjeosero).

This painting is the property of West Point Military Academy. It shows a Waffen-SS NCO wearing the camouflaged smock, fall-side out, armed with a Bergmann MP35/I machine pistol, frequently encountered in SS-Kampfgruppe Nord. (DR)

After thorough preparation during June and July and with a heavy opening artillery barrage, the *Gruppe* attacked the Nyatovara Heights on August 1. On the 2nd, the heights dominating Njato-Wara were "*in deustcher Hand*," despite a network of effective defensive positions in primary forest covered by heavy, preregistered mortar fire, and vigorous Soviet counterattacks. During August, 7.GD, finally reunited, was deployed as an advanced guard between the Kiestinski–Louhi road and Lake

The Brandenburgers were experts in deep-penetration patrols. One company, by way of example— the "15.(leichte)," then "Trommsdorf" after its commanding officer, a second lieutenant—deployed to Finland in early 1942. The men came from mountainous regions and their equipment was adapted to their missions: Finnish boat-like sledges (*akjas*) for winter and inflatable dinghies for the summer, "polar" dogs, and rifles (with or without silencers and telescopic sights), and recoilless LG40 guns. Their acclimatization was supported by the Finns. However, their first engagement, in April 1942, was a failure. Honor was saved in June, thanks to their commando raids in the interval sectors along the almost overwhelmed German positions to the north of Kietinski.

Top, a position that it held until late 1943. Its defense was organized in depth, almost through 360° (though the main effort was directed eastward), with preregistered heavy mortar fire patterns covering all sectors.

Geb.-Pz.Jg.Abt 99 was subsequently immediately subordinated to Gruppe Nord as soon as it arrived on May 19. On August 8, the Soviets tried, unsuccessfully, to take the Kangaswara Heights behind the less-fortified German second line, covered by I./GJR218 positions. Several other raids were made in the following weeks, all driven off. The forest offered few opportunities for observation and only patrols and "doorbells" revealed the attempts. The lakes and swamps offered wider fields for observation but prevented almost any form of maneuver. The division was not inactive, of course, with the *Jagdkommandos* also launching probing attacks.

The first snow arrived bringing reinforcement in the way of Ski-Btl 82 (Captain Fischer's ski battalion) to continue harassing operations and to react more effectively to the probing attacks by Soviet skiers, who traversed the snow-covered frozen lakes with ease. The winter terrain, indeed, favored larger-scale Soviet operations.

A propaganda postcard shows Kampfgruppe Nord during one of its earliest Finnish engagements. (Luftwaffe Museum Archives)

Appendix 1: Organization Chart

Units	Date created	Jäger	Artillerie	Pioniere	Organic Units (others)	Observations
WEHRMACHT HEER						
20.Geb.-A	04.07.1942	Grp. Rossi, DivGrp. Kräutler: GJR139, JgBtl3	GAA 124	Geb.-Werfer-Abt. 10		
1.GD	09.04.1938 20.11.1943	GJR 98, 99, 100* GJR 98 and 99, GJB 54	GAR 79		Geb.PzJAbt 44 Others: 54	* Left 1.GD after the French campaign and took part in making up 5.GD
2.GD	01.04.1938	GJR 136, 137	GAR 111	GPiBtl82	GebAA 11 then 111 GebPzJgAbt 47 then 55 Others: 67	
3.GD 3.GD	01.04.1938 02.03.1942	GJR 138, 13 GJR 138, 144	GAR 112 GAR 112	GPiBtl 83 GPiBtl 83	GebAA 12 then 112 GebPzJgAbt 48 RadfAbt95, GebPzJg Abt95 Others: 68	
4.GD	23.10.1940	GJR 13, 91	GAR 94		94	
5.GD	25.10.1940	GJR 85, 100	GAR 95		GPzJgAbt 85, GAA 85 Others: 95	
6.GD	01.06.1940	GJR 141, 143	GAR 118		GPzJgAbt 47, GAA 112 Others: 91	
7.GD	15.11.1941	GJR 206, 218, SchiBtl82	GAR 82	GPiBtl 82	99	
157.Res.D 157.GD	01.10.1944	ResGJR1 GJR 296, 297	GebArtAbt79 /ResAR7 GAR 1057		1057	
8.GD	02.1945	GJR 296, 297	GAR 1057		GPzJgAbt 157, Others 1057	From 157.GD
9.GD Nord	03.1945	DivGrp Kräutler				07.09.44 "Div zbV 140"
KpfGr Semmering KpfGr Raithel 9.GD Ost	03.1945 25.04.1945	GJ-Unterführerschule, SS-GebJg-Ers.-Btl Leoben, pers. of the Kpf-Geschwader Bölcke	GebArt.-Schule Dachstein			9.GD « Ost » from the Kpfgr Raithel and the Geb.Jäger-Div. « Steiermark » (Schatten-Div.)
Div. Nr 188 188.ResGD 188.GD	05.11.1939 08.10.1943 01.03.1944	GJErsR136,138,139 ResGJR 136 to 139 GJR 901 to 904	ResGArtAbt I and II/112 GAR 1088	RGPiBtl 83 GPiB 1088	1088 1088	
139.GJBrigade	05.06.1944	3 x GJB	GAAbt 124			Subord 3.GD then DivGrp "Kräutler" then 1945 "Generaloberst Dietl"
1.SJB 1.SJD	09.1943 02.06.1944	SJR1 and 2, schw. SBtl1 SJR1 and 2	AR152 and schw. Werfer-Btl 18	SkiPiBtl85	Ski-Füs.Btl 1 Others: 152	

Units	Date created	Jäger	Artillerie	Pioniere	Organic Units (others)	Observations
97.JgD	28.06.1944	JgR 204 and 207	AR 81		97	AR 81 mountain equipped partly Ersatz of the GebArt
IR 499	26.08.1939	ErsGJR 137, 138 and 139				
91.(LL) ID then 15.11.44 344.ID	15.01.1944 then reorg. 15.04.1944		GAR 191			I./ and II./ equipped with GebH 40
Heeres-GJB 201 I./GJR 137	09.10.1944 03.1945					Army organic unit then 2.GD
Heeres-GJB 202	09.10.1944					Army organic unit disbanded 03.1945
28.JgD	01.12.1941		GAR 28 with I. and II.(Geb)/ ***			In 1941, 28(le) ID with medium mountain equipment
"Rgt Treeck"	19.07.1944 10.1944				Organic unit WK XVIII	
WAFFEN-SS						
6.SS Nord	09.1942 then reorg. 22.10.1943	GJR 7 then 11 "R.H." GJR 6 then 12 "M.G."	GAR« Nord » then 6	GpiBtl 6	6	R.H.: Reinhard Heydrich M.G.: Michael Gaissmair
7.SS Prinz Eugen	10.1942 then reorg. 22.10.1943	GJR 1 then 13 GJR 2 then 14	GAR 7	GPiBtl 7	7**	** of which a Pz-Abt « PE» to a PzKp equipped with captured French matériel then Sturmgeschütze
13.SS Handschar	30.04.1943 then reorg. 06.1944	GJR 1 then 27 GJR 2 then 28	GAR 13	GPiBtl 13	13	
21.SS Skanderbeg	01.05.1944	GJR 50, 51	GAR 21	GPiBtl 21	21	
23.SS Kama	10.06.1944	GJR 55, 56	GAR 23	GPiBtl 23	24	
24.SS Karstjäger	01.08.1944	Waffen-GJR 59	I/GAR 24	GPiBtl 24 (1x Kp)	24	
MISCELLANEOUS						
10. Armee				GPi-Btl 818		
19. Armee	01.1945		Heeres-GAAbt 669			
90.PzGrenDiv	23.10.1943	GJKp 190				
Polizei-GJR 18 SS-PolGJR 18***	07.1942 24.02.1943					**** Change of denomination of all the Polizei Rgt.
FOREIGN UNITS: See Chapter "The Eastern Front, 1941–42"						
*** Others JgD (101, 118) had artillery groups equipped with mountain matériel, but without the regiments being denominated « Geb. »						

Appendix 2: Tactical Symbols

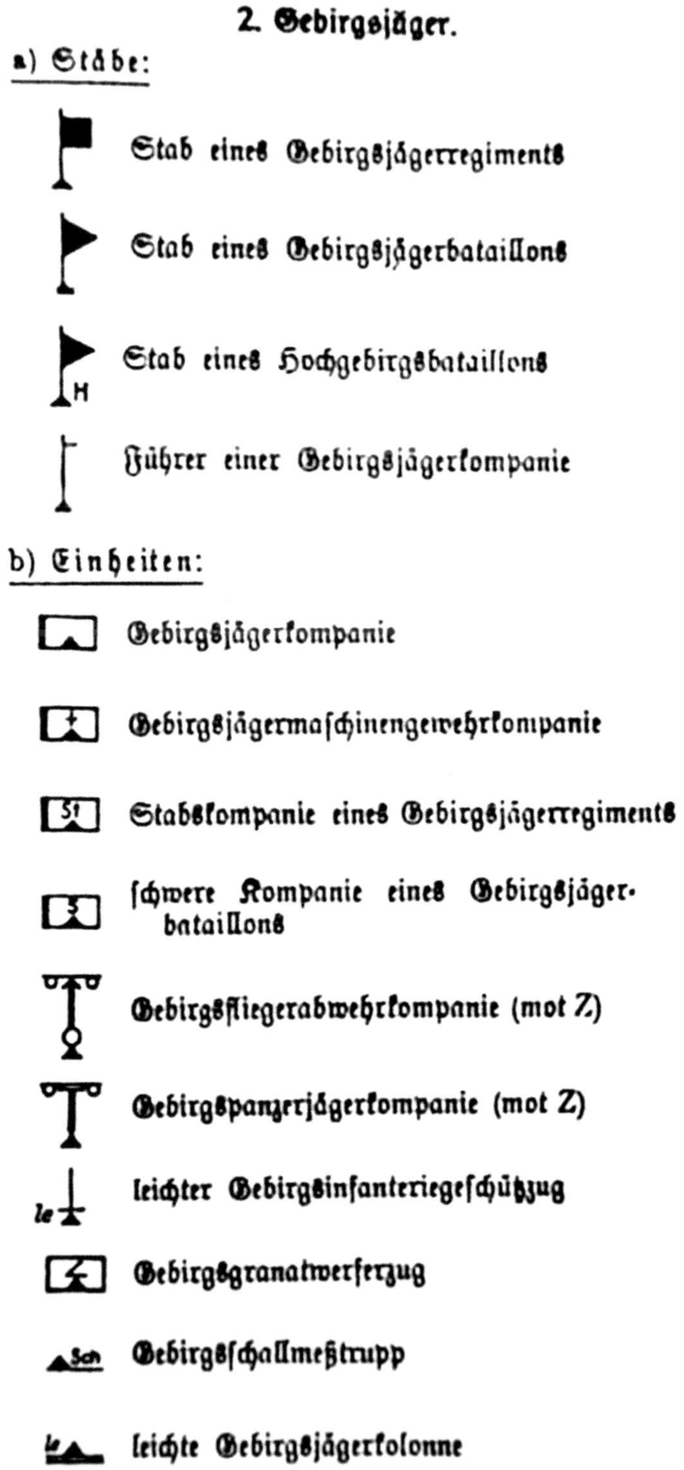

2. Gebirgsjäger.

a) Stäbe:

Stab eines Gebirgsjägerregiments

Stab eines Gebirgsjägerbataillons

H Stab eines Hochgebirgsbataillons

Führer einer Gebirgsjägerkompanie

b) Einheiten:

Gebirgsjägerkompanie

Gebirgsjägermaschinengewehrkompanie

St Stabskompanie eines Gebirgsjägerregiments

schwere Kompanie eines Gebirgsjäger-bataillons

Gebirgsfliegerabwehrkompanie (mot Z)

Gebirgspanzerjägerkompanie (mot Z)

le leichter Gebirgsinfanteriegeschützzug

Gebirgsgranatwerferzug

Sch Gebirgsschallmeßtrupp

le leichte Gebirgsjägerkolonne

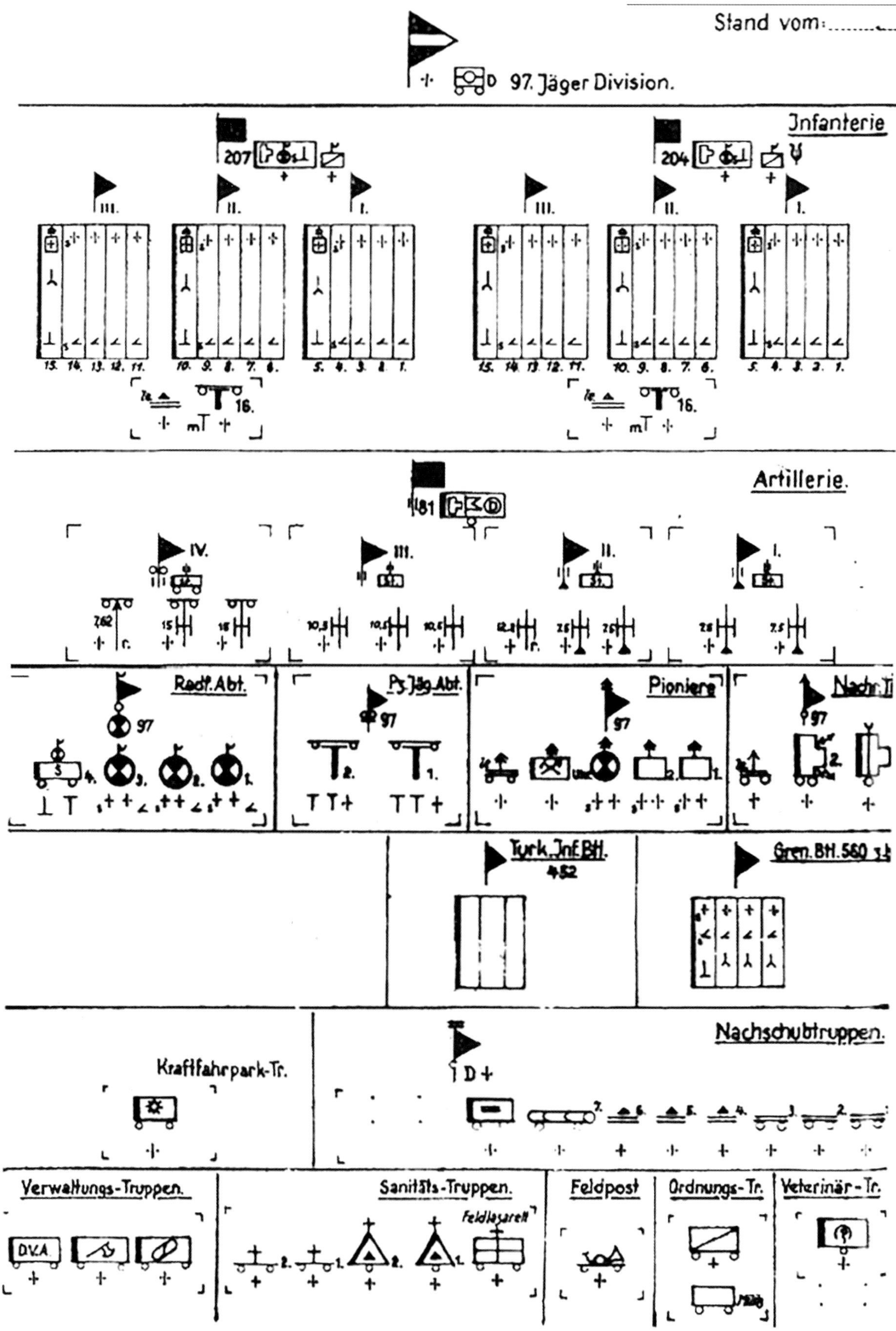
Stand vom:
97. Jäger Division.
Infanterie
207
204
III.
II.
I.
16.
Artillerie.
181
IV.
III.
II.
I.
Radf. Abt.
97
Pz. Jäg. Abt.
97
Pioniere
97
Nachr. T
97
Turk. Inf. Btl.
452
Gren. Btl. 560
Nachschubtruppen.
Kraftfahrpark-Tr.
Verwaltungs-Truppen.
D.V.A.
Sanitäts-Truppen.
Feldlasarett
Feldpost
Ordnungs-Tr.
Veterinär-Tr.

Kriegsgliederung der 1. Gebirgs-Division
am 9.5.40

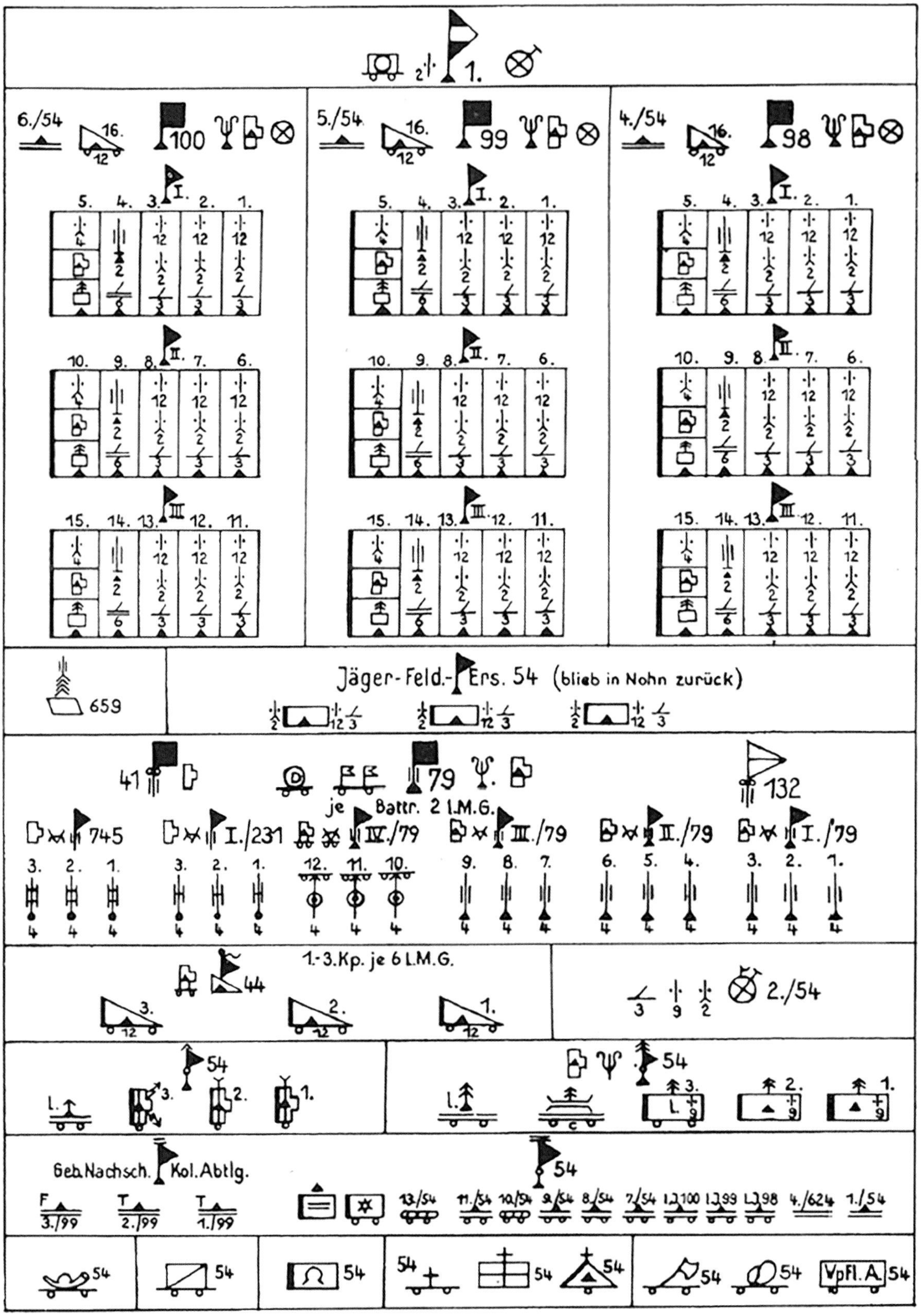

Appendix 3: Abbreviations

Abteilung (*Abt.*): detachment, group, battalion (depending on the arm and the level of command)
Alpenjäger: mountain chasseur (Austrian)
Armeeoberkommando (*AOK*): Army headquarters (staff and support units)
Bataillon (*Btl.*, *Btlen.* plural): battalion
Batterie (*Bttr.*): battery
bergfähig: fit for mountain operations
Brigade (*Brig.*): brigade
Funk (*Fu.*): radio
Gebirgsarmee (*GebA* or *GA*): mountain army
Gebirgsartillerie (*GebArt*): mountain artillery
Gebirgsartillerie-Abteilung (*G.A.A.*): mountain artillery battalion
Gebirgsartillerie-Regiment (*G.A.R.*): mountain artillery regiment
Gebirgsaufklärer (*GebAufkl.*): mountain reconnaissance (recce)
Gebirgs-Aufklärungs-Abteilung (*Geb.-A.A.*): mountain recce battalion
Gebirgsbrigade (*GebBrig, G.B.*): mountain brigade
Gebirgsdivision (*GebDiv, G.D.*): mountain division (*GDen* in the plural)
Gebirgsjäger (*GebJg, GJ*): mountain chasseur
Gebirgsjäger-Regiment (*G.J.R., GJR*): mountain chasseur regiment
Gebirgskorps or *Gebirgs-Armeekorps* (*GAK*): mountain army corps
Gebirgsnachrichten [(*Geb*) *N.A.*]: mountain signals
Gebirgspanzerjäger (*Geb.Pz.Jg.*) or *Gebirgspanzerabwehr* (*Geb.Pz.Abw.*): mountain antitank destroyer
Gebirgspionier [(*Geb.*)*Pi.*]: mountain engineer
Gebirgsträger: mountain porter
Jäger (*Jg.*): chasseur
Kolonne (*Kol.*): column
Kompanie (*Komp., Kp.*): company
Kriegstagebuch (*KTB*): war diary
Leicht (*le.*): light
Maschinengewehr (*MG*): machine gun
Minenwerfer (*M.W.*): mortars
Regiment (*Rgt., Rgter.* plural): regiment
Sanitäts (*San.*): medical service
Schwer (*schw.*): heavy
Schwadron: squadron
Spiess: adjutant
Sturm: assault
Sturmgeschütz: assault gun
Train (Austrian *Kraftfahrer)*: baggage train
Tross: combat train
Zug: section/platoon

Sources

Aichner, Ernst (Hrsg.), *Deutsche Gebirgstruppen, vom 1. Weltkrieg bis zur Gegenwart*, Sonderaustellung des bayerischen Armeemuseums Ingolstadt, 1983.

Béraud, Henri, *Bataille des Alpes*, Album Mémorial Juin 1940–1944/45, Editions Heimdal, Bayeux, 1987.

Bernage, Georges & François de Lannoy, *Dictionnaire historique: Les divisions de l'Armée de Terre allemande*, Editions Heimdal, 1997.

Bernage, Georges & François de Lannoy, *Dictionnaire historique: La Luftwaffe et la Waffen-SS, 1939–1945*, Editions Heimdal, 1998.

Buchner, Alex, *Kampf im Gebirge*, Schild Verlag GmbH, München-Lochhausen, 1957.

Department of the Army Pamphlet NO 20-292, *Warfare in the Far North*, Department of the Army, Washington DC, 1951.

Des Hautes-Alpes à Narvik, mai-juin 1940: le 14° Bataillon de Chasseurs Alpins en Scandinavie, CNDP/CDDP de Gap.

Die deutschen Gebirgsdivisionen im zweiten Weltkrieg, Allgemeine schweizerische Militärzeitschrift (ASMZ), 1948.

Greiner, Helmut & Percy Ernst Schramm, *Kriegstagebuch des Oberkommandos der Wehrmacht 1939–1945*, Bernard und Graefe Verlag, München, 1982.

Haupt, Werner, *Leningrad Wochow Kurland: Bildbericht der Heeresgruppe Nord 1941–1945*, Podzun-Pallas-Verlag, Friedberg, 1976.

Hoffmann, Heinrich, *Für Hitler bis Narvik*, Verlag Heinrich Hoffmann, München 13, 1941.

Kaltenegger Roland, *Ludwig Kübler: General der Gebirgstruppe*, Motorbuch Verlag, Stuttgart, 1998.

Kaltenegger, Roland, *Die Geschichte der deutschen Gebirgstruppe 1915 bis heute*, Motorbuch Verlag, Stuttgart, 1980.

Keegan, John (ed.) & *The Times*, *Atlas de la Seconde Guerre mondiale*, France Loisirs, Paris, 1990.

Kern, Erich, *Generalfeldmarschall Schörner*, Verlag, K.W. Schütz KG, Preuβich Oldendorf, 1976.

Knabe, Konrad, *Die schweigende Front: Dietl's Kampf im hohen Norden 1940–1944*, Druffel-Verlag, Leoni am Starnberger See, 1979.

Kosar, Franz, *Gebirgsartillerie: Geschichte, Waffen, Organisation*, Motorbuch Verlag, Stuttgart, 1987

Lanz, Hubert, *Gebirgsjäger: Die 1. Gebirgsdivision 1935–1945*, Verlag Hans-Henning Podzun, Bad Nauheim, 1954.

Levsen, Dirk, *Krieg im Norden: Die Kämpfe in Norwegen 1940*, Verlag E. S. Mittler & Sohn GmbH, Hamburg-Berlin-Bonn, 2000.

Offizier im grossdeutschen Heer, Merkworte für die Berufswahl, Kriegsausgabe, 1942.

Ott, Ernst-Ludwig, *Die Spielhahnjäger 1940–1945, Bilddokumentation der 97. Jäger-Division*, Podzun-Pallas-Verlag, 1982.

Ott, Ernst-Ludwig, *Jäger am Feind: Geschichte und Opfergang der 97. Jäger-Division*, Selbstverlag der Kameradschaft der Spielhahnjäger e.V., München, 1966.

Ringel, Julius, *Hurra, die Gams!: Ein Gedenkbuch für die Soldaten der 5. Gebirgsdivision*, Leopold Stocker Verlag, Graz et Göttingen, 1975.

Schlicht, Adolf & Jürgen Kraus, *Die Uniformierung und Ausrüstung des deutschen Reichsheeres 1919–1932*, Bayerisches Armeemuseum Ingolstadt, 1987.

Schmitz, Peter & Klaus-Jürgen Thies, *Die Truppenkennzeichen der Verbände und Einheiten der deutschen Wehrmacht und Waffen-SS im Zweiten Weltkrieg 1939–1945*, Biblio Verlag, Osnabrück, 2000.

Schuler, Emil, *Mit dem Bergschuh in Russland und Finnland. Kriegserlebnisse und Kriegserfahrungen der 7. Gebirgs-Division bearbeitet von Emil Schuler*, Eigenverlag Emil Schuler Leinen, 1959.

Später, Helmut, *Die Brandenburger: Eine deutsche Kommandotruppe zbV 800*, Verlagsagentur Walther Angerer, München 86, 1978.

Steurich, Alfred, *Gebirgsjäger im Bild: 6. SS Gebirgsdivision Nord 1940–1945*, Munin-Verlag GmbH, Osnabrück, 1976.

Tessin, Georg, *Verbände und Truppen der deutschen Wehrmacht und Waffen-SS im Zweiten Weltkrieg 1939–1945* Osnabrück, 1977–80.

Thomas, Nigel, Carlos Caballero Jurado & Simon McCouaig, *Wehrmacht Auxiliary Forces*, Men-At-Arms Series, Osprey Military, 1992.

Thomas, Nigel, Krunoslav Mikulan & Darko Pavlović, *Axis Forces in Yugoslavia 1941–45*, Men-at-Arms Series, Osprey Military, 1995.

Von Clausewitz, Carl, *Vom Kriege*.

Von Hrsg. Oberkommando der Wehrmacht, *Kampf um Norwegen, Oberkommando der Wehrmacht*, Zeitgeschichte—Verlag Wilhelm Andermann, Berlin W 35, 1940.

Von Oven, Wilfred & Jürgen Hahn-Butry, *Panzer am Balkan*, Wilhelm Limpert Verlag, Berlin, 1941.

Weinberger, Andreas, *Das gelbe Edelweiss*, Zentralverlag der NSDAP, Franz Eher Nachfolger, GmbH, München, 1943.

Wetzig, Sonja, *Die Stalin-Linie 1941*, Podzun-Pallas-Verlag, Wölfersheim-Berstadt, 1997.

Zorn, Major, *Von Drontheim nach Narvik: Das Büffel-Unternehmen*, AOK Norwegen, 1940.

Periodicals

39–45 Magazine various issues.

Der Landser various issues.

Die Gebirgstruppe, Federation of the German Mountain Troops' Association, various issues including a 1957 special edition.

Die Wehrmacht various issues.

Historica various issues.

La Domenica del Corriere various issues.

La Gazette des Uniformes various issues.

Militaria Magazine various issues.

Nordruf various issues.

Signal various issues.

Soldat und Waffe–Der II. Weltkrieg, Jahr-Verlag KG, 2000 Hamburg 1.

Tempo various issues.

Waffen-Revue various issues.

Index